# GHOST TOWNS
## of the SOUTHWEST

Your Guide to the Historic Mining Camps
& Ghost Towns of Arizona and New Mexico

Text by Jim Hinckley
Photography by Kerrick James

Voyageur Press

First published in 2010 by Voyageur Press, an imprint of MBI Publishing Company, 400 First Avenue North, Suite 300, Minneapolis, MN 55401 USA

Voyageur Press titles are also available at discounts in bulk quantity for industrial or sales-promotional use. For details write to Special Sales Manager at MBI Publishing Company, 400 First Avenue North, Suite 300, Minneapolis, MN 55401 USA.

To find out more about our books, visit us online at www.voyageurpress.com.

Library of Congress Cataloging-in-Publication Data

Hinckley, James, 1958-
Ghost towns of the Southwest: your guide to the historic mining camps and ghost towns of Arizona and New Mexico / text by Jim Hinckley; photography by Kerrick James.
           p. cm.
Includes index.
ISBN 978-0-7603-3221-4 (sb : alk. paper)
1. Ghost towns—Arizona—Guidebooks. 2. Ghost towns—New Mexico—Guidebooks. 3. Mining camps—Arizona—Guidebooks. 4. Mining camps—New Mexico—Guidebooks. 5. Arizona—Guidebooks. 6. New Mexico—Guidebooks. I. James, Kerrick. II. Title.
F812.H56 2010
917.91—dc22

                            2009023427

ISBN-13: 978-0-7603-3221-4

Editor: Amy Glaser
Design Manager: LeAnn Kuhlmann
Cartographer: Patti Isaacs, Parrot Graphics
Series Designer: Cindy Samargia Laun
Layout Designer: Cindy Samargia Laun
Cover Designer: John Barnett / 4 Eyes Design

Printed in China

*Frontispiece:* OK Corral Shootout Graves, Tombstone, Arizona.
*Title page:* Spider Rock, Canyon de Chelly, Arizona.
*Title page inset:* Living room, Strafford Hotel, Shakespeare, New Mexico.

# CONTENTS

# INTRODUCTION

Arizona and New Mexico make up a large portion of the Southwest. More than 234,000 square miles of amazing geographic and geologic diversity; stark, sterile desert plains; towering snow-capped mountains; deep red rock canyons where thundering waterfalls spill into turquoise blue pools; and alpine meadows bordered by forests of towering pines are contained within these man-made borders.

For centuries, these gorgeous landscapes have served as the backdrop for a cavalcade of human history. Almost a thousand years before Columbus sailed the ocean blue, the Anasazi built cities that were engineering marvels among the towering canyon walls here. The Hohokam built villages in the fertile soils of the desert river valleys and transformed the surrounding arid lands into a paradise with the masterful development of an irrigation system that lasted long after their settlements had disappeared from the horizon.

The Spanish Conquistadors came in search of gold and souls, brought "civilization" to the ancestors of the Anasazi, and built villages of their own, often on the ruins of those that came before. With the passing of years, the winds of time reclaimed many of these.

*Above:* With Castle Dome as a backdrop, this old ore car is a fitting memorial for a town whose mining history spans more than a century.

*Opposite:* Vestiges from more than a century of mining litter the rugged and scenic landscapes of the Cerbat Mountains in northwestern Arizona.

American traders, explorers, and adventurers seeking a faster route to the gold fields of California rolled west and discovered unexpected treasures along the way. Fueled by fortunes of pelts and gold, silver and empires of cattle, timber and the railroad, a new wave of towns and cities sprang from the rugged lands.

Isolated desert valleys became modern, bustling metropolises in mere weeks and became as empty as the Anasazi canyon homes just as quickly. More than a few of these towns are immortalized as legends forever associated with larger-than-life figures: Tombstone and Wyatt Earp, Lincoln and Billy the Kid, and Fairbank and Jeff Milton.

Over time, the dusty desert winds reclaimed the valleys, and time swept the names of once prosperous communities from the map, as well as memory. Soon only picturesque ruins and legends remained.

A few villages that survived as shadows of their former glory found new life in new booms. Others clung to life as an outpost in a harsh land for a new breed of adventurers: motorists. In time, many of these villages succumbed to the changing times, and another sea of ghost towns dotted the desert plains.

Today the ruins framed by majestic scenery and breathtaking landscapes stand in silent testimony to the power of hopes and dreams. The towns that cling to life with dust swirling along once busy thoroughfares and those that remain as faint traces in the desert sands lure visitors with scenic wonder, tangible links to a colorful history, or the prospect of lost treasure.

As you seek these lost worlds, remember those who once called them home and give thought to those who will follow your visit. Take nothing but photographs and memories; leave nothing but footprints. Plan your trips carefully. Many of these town sites are in very remote locations and summer temperatures in the desert often exceed 110 degrees. Mine shafts and tunnels are unstable and should be approached with extreme caution.

Last but not least, please watch out for snakes. Snakes seek cooler places in the opening of tunnels, under rocks, and in crevasses to escape the heat so be careful where you step or place your hands.

*Opposite top:* The historic Brown Store in White Oaks has been pulled back from the precipice of abandonment and is one of the few remnants of a once-thriving business district.

*Opposite bottom:* These steel headframes from Kelly's glory days as a mining boom town date from the twentieth century.

# GHOSTS OF
# NORTHWEST
# ARIZONA

YOUR BASE CAMP FOR THE EXPLORATION OF GHOST TOWNS in northwest Arizona is Kingman, a historic community with a long and colorful history. Access to all towns and town sites in this portion of the state are easy day trips from Kingman, although a few trips will require the use of a high-profile or four-wheel-drive vehicle.

These towns include a frontier-era mining community preserved in a circa 1930 state of arrested decay, a mining town saved from abandonment with the resurgent interest in Route 66, and another mining community almost erased from the map with the modern bane of many old towns—open-pit mining. Other gems include two former county seats and a railroad town that also has ties to legendary Route 66.

Beautiful blooms are in the foreground of the hills of Oatman.

In Cerbat, Arizona, it takes a keen eye to find the vestiges of the old town's glory days. The remnants are quickly being reclaimed by the desert.

*Lake Mead*

Colorado River

Boulder
City

ARIZONA

NEVADA

BLACK MTS.

WHITE HILLS

145
White Hills
Road

BLACK MESA

93

Colorado River

CERBAT MTS.

CHLORIDE

Grasshopper Junction     125

Mineral
Park Road

HACKBERRY

66

MINERAL PARK

PEACOCK
MTS.

CERBAT

68

Kingman     40

Backcountry
Byway Historic
Route 66/
Oatman Highway

Bullhead City

GOLDROAD

95

Boundary
Cone Road     OATMAN

HUALAPAI MTS.

AQUARIUS MTS.

Mohave Valley

40

95

93

WIKIEUP

95

Signal Road

Lake Havasu City

SIGNAL

CALIFORNIA

| 0 | | | | 25 Miles |
|---|---|---|---|---|

| 0 | | | | 25 Kilometers |
|---|---|---|---|---|

# OATMAN

Oatman, located on the western flanks of the rocky Black Mountains above the Colorado River, is a relative newcomer in northwest Arizona. The town dates to 1902 when Ben Taddock made a significant gold discovery in the shadow of the looming Elephant's Tooth, a distinctive rock formation. With the sale of the property to the Vivian Mining Company in 1903, development of the mines and the mining camp began to proceed at a rapid clip.

Within two years, the community, then called Vivian, consisted of a very active chamber of commerce, two banks, several stores, and a population of more than one hundred. The community was renamed Oatman in 1909, a year after the next big gold deposit discovery and the subsequent formation of the Tom Reed Mining Company.

*Above:* The Oatman Hotel is the largest adobe structure in Mohave County. It is also where Clark Gable and Carole Lombard spent their first night as husband and wife.

*Opposite:* Elephant's Tooth is the name of the unique rock formation that towers over Oatman.

On February 18, 1851, the family of Royce Oatman was traveling west, alone, on the Gila Trail when a party of Yavapai or Tonto Apache overran the small wagon train. The lone survivors were Olive, twelve; Mary Ann, eight; and Lorenzo, the oldest son who was clubbed and left for dead.

The sisters were taken captive and later traded to a band of Mojave Indians and received surprisingly decent treatment, though Mary Ann did not survive the ordeal of native life in the mountains that border the Colorado River Valley. As was the custom of Mojave women, Olive was tattooed on the chin. Lorenzo survived, moved to California, and hoped to some day find his sisters.

In 1856, Henry Grinnell of Fort Yuma secured the freedom of a white captive living among the Mojave Indians with an exchange of trade goods. The joyous reunion of Olive with her brother several months later garnered attention in newspapers throughout the country. The remainder of her life was relatively anticlimactic; she married, raised a family, and died quietly at the age of sixty-four.

Traffic on Route 66 became the livelihood for Oatman in the 1930s as production at the area mines declined. *Mohave County Historical Society*

The speculation is that the name change was in honor of Olive Oatman, a young girl who was kidnapped near Gila Bend in 1851, traded to Mojave Indians, and was subsequently rescued near the town site. A secondary story added the element of a son; it stemmed from a man who prospected in the area and claimed to be the son of Olive.

The town began to boom thanks to the opening of the United Eastern Mine in 1913 and the National Old Trails Highway in 1914, predecessor to Route 66. Estimates place the population at several thousand during its peak in the early 1930s.

Over the years, the town has had several brushes with fame. In 1914 Barney Oldfield and Louis Chevrolet, as well as a half dozen other drivers, roared through town in the last of the Desert Classic Cactus Derby races. In the late 1930s, Clark Gable and Carole Lombard, after marrying in Kingman, spent an evening at the Oatman Hotel, the largest adobe structure still standing in Mohave County.

The distinctive rock formations and the picturesque Black Mountains that loom above the town, as well as its scattering of weathered buildings, present the illusion that Oatman is a movie set, which is exactly what it was on several occasions. The most notable movies filmed here were *Foxfire* in 1955, *Edge of Eternity* in 1959, *How the West Was Won* in 1962, and *Roadhouse 66* in 1984.

Oatman's population dwindled to less than fifty in the 1950s as a result of mine closures in 1942 and the realignment of Route 66 in 1953, but the old town has experienced a new boom with resurging interest in Route 66. Although only a handful of original buildings remain, the re-created storefronts, narrow main street (Route 66) crowded with traffic, free-roaming burros, and throngs of tourists provide a fair picture of what it was like in its heyday.

## WHEN YOU GO

*Oatman is located 32 miles southwest of Kingman on the original Route 66 alignment. The last 9 miles are not for the faint of heart, as these are the steepest grades and sharpest curves found anywhere on Route 66. For vehicles such as trucks with trailers and motor homes, access is via Boundary Cone Road that connects Oatman with State Highway 95.*

# GOLDROAD

It takes a vivid imagination to see a vibrant community in the scattered ruins and assorted rock-strewn roads that wind into the surrounding canyons or extensive mine tailings near Goldroad. With the recent reopening and development of the primary mine here, this becomes an even more difficult exercise.

Goldroad, as with Oatman, is a relative newcomer in the annals of Arizona mining towns. It dates back to 1899, when Jose Jerez stumbled on a surprisingly rich vein of gold while rounding up burros that had strayed from his camp in the Black Mountains. Similar finds—dating back to 1863 when John Moss began a small mine—had sparked short spurts of mining and exploration in the area, but Jerez's discovery was different in several aspects.

First, Jerez had the financial backing of Henry Lovin, a successful Kingman merchant who often grubstaked prospectors but seldom saw return on the investment. Second, this find proved to be precursor to a substantial lode of low-grade ore that would have been unprofitable to mine at an earlier time.

In 1901, Jerez sold his share in the property and faded into obscurity. Lovin sold his interest in the property too, but he made a fortune with general merchandise stores and a freight company that served the community of Acme (renamed Goldroad in 1906), as well as Oatman and Kingman.

More than seven million dollars in gold was extracted from deep tunnels hewn from the hard rock at the Goldroad Mine between 1903 and 1931. Smaller mines, a mill, and service facilities that met the needs of motorists on the National Old Trails Highway, and later Route 66, ensured the community of about four hundred people was prosperous and busy.

The S-curve on Route 66, which enters the town from the east, is the sharpest on this historic highway. Buses utilized a clearing at the curve, as it

## WHEN YOU GO

*The town site of Goldroad is located 30 miles southwest of Kingman, about 2 miles east of Oatman, on historic Route 66. The road from east or west is narrow and very steep with sharp curves.*

Goldroad consists of stark vestiges from a century of mining framed by the rugged Black Mountains.

The truck had replaced the mule by the mid-1910s, but transporting supplies through the Black Mountains to Goldroad was still a daunting endeavor. *Mohave County Historical Society*

was too sharp for them to make the turn. One enterprising garage owner offered, for a fee, a driver for those too intimidated to traverse the grades over the Black Mountains.

Remnants of the original alignment of the highway, which is also the National Old Trails Highway, are still visible in the canyon below the current highway and just above the town site. This would have been the route followed during the 1914 Desert Classic Cactus Derby.

The closure of the mines just before World War II, the realignment of the highway in 1953, and a state tax law that encouraged mine owners to dismantle abandoned buildings were the death knell for the community. By the mid-1960s, little remained other than mine tailings, the concrete foundations of the mill, assorted stone, and adobe ruins.

Today, with the high price of gold, a large section of the town site is off limits as efforts are under way to reopen the mines. A number of ruins still front the highway and nestle in the picturesque canyons that frame the small valley.

# WHITE HILLS

Legend has it that Hualapai Jeff was in search of iron oxide to use as face paint for a tribal ritual when he discovered a rich specimen of silver in 1891. When Judge Henry Shaffer of Gold Basin saw the specimen, he and two friends, John Burnett and John Sullivan, set out with Hualapai Jeff to evaluate the find, or so the story goes.

Scars on the harsh desert landscapes offer a hint that White Hills was once the largest town in Mohave County and a community with a bright future.

As news of the rich strike spread throughout the surrounding territories, prospectors flooded into the area, and a Denver-based syndicate bought up the principal claims, imported the most modern mining equipment, and established a mill. By early summer of 1892, the town consisted of two hundred residents and a number of stores, restaurants, and saloons.

White Hills faced two major problems from its inception. Water was a scarce commodity that sold for one dollar a barrel. The second was that the ore bodies were sporadic in nature, with pockets running in excess of two thousand ounces to the ton with the remainder being of the poorest grade.

In 1894, the acquisition of the primary claims and mines by an English conglomerate that drilled deep wells and ran miles of pipe from springs in the surrounding mountains solved the community's water problems. This in turn fueled White Hills' growth, and by 1895, the population had risen to more than one thousand, making it the largest town in Mohave County.

It was also one of the most modern towns in the area. Residents enjoyed the relative luxury of electric lights, telephone service, running water, and indoor plumbing.

By 1910, the profitability of mining the poor ore grades resulted in curtailed productivity. White Hills began a precipitous slide from which it never recovered. In 1914, the population had dropped to such a degree a post office was no longer sustainable.

Today little remains of White Hills with the exception of scattered foundations, mine tailings, the imposing ruins of the mill, and desert scenery. Recent real estate development in the area threatens to erase even these faint traces.

## WHEN YOU GO

*White Hills is located approximately 48 miles northwest of Kingman. From Kingman, drive north on U.S. Highway 93 about 35 miles. Turn north on White Hills Road, and continue for 13 miles.*

Claim markers stand as silent sentinels to the scarce remnants and faint traces of White Hills that remain on the rock-strewn desert plain.

# CHLORIDE

Chloride dates to the discovery of a deposit of silver chloride in the early 1860s and is the oldest surviving mining camp in the Cerbat Mountains. Tucked into the foothills of those towering mountains, it is also one of the most scenic mining camps.

The remote location initially required ore to be shipped overland to Hardyville, where it then traveled down the Colorado River by steamboat to the Gulf of Mexico and Pacific Ocean, and then to England by ship for milling. This extended travel route, as well as persistent problems with the native Hualapai Indians, limited the development of the mines until a mill was built in Mineral Park in the 1870s and the railroad line to nearby Kingman was completed in 1883.

For the next fifteen years, Chloride enjoyed a steady growth of both residents and businesses. In 1898, this prosperity led the Arizona & Utah Railroad to build a spur line across the Sacramento Valley to connect with the Santa Fe Railroad main line at McConnico, which is south of Kingman.

Great fanfare and celebration commemorated the arrival of the railroad in Chloride. Incorporation followed this stellar event, which made Chloride the first community in Mohave County to do so.

A gas station ringed by train tracks survives on the main street of Chloride.

The Arizona Central Bank holds its own against the elements.

Throughout the first decades of the new century, Chloride entered a period of stability, even though the railroad proved to be a short-lived venture. The town's population was near two thousand at its peak.

The mine closures that started in the 1930s escalated into the 1940s and culminated with the closure of the Tennessee-Schuylkill, one of the deepest mines in Arizona, in 1947. The highway was rerouted around the town during the same time period and that proved to be the proverbial straw that broke the camel's back. The town quickly settled into a quiet, sleepy existence.

Today, Chloride is a delightful little village of more than one hundred retirees, crusty desert rats, and eccentric artists. Two pleasant cafés, several gift shops, a combination market/museum/gift shop, a post office, and a bar constitute the business district. The best way to enjoy Chloride is on foot. Stroll the dusty streets and give your imagination free reign.

There are vestiges from the glory days on almost every street. Among the most picturesque are the railroad depot, a 1930s service station, a motel complex that now houses a café and art gallery, the jail, the post office, and the Tennessee Saloon. A quiet cemetery is located south of town and offers wonderful views of the valley.

## WHEN YOU GO

*From Kingman, drive 18 miles north on U.S. Highway 93. Turn northeast on County Road 125 and drive 4 miles. The first four-way stop will be the central business district of Chloride.*

# MINERAL PARK

Indications are that the earliest mining activity in the area of Mineral Park pre-dated the community by centuries. Native Americans at several locations in the surrounding canyons mined rich deposits of turquoise for use locally and as a lucrative trading commodity with tribes as far away as the Zuni pueblos.

The modern mining era dates to the late 1860s with the filing of several claims and the establishment of limited mining activity. By 1871, the rich deposits of gold and silver had attracted large investment conglomerates that erected a five stamp mill and laid out a town site.

The narrow canyon quickly became a beehive of activity with more than two hundred men employed in the mines, building adobe and timber structures and grading lots. By December 1872, Mineral Park had mushroomed to such a point it could support numerous saloons, a post office, several stores, and a school.

Its central location in the rich Cerbat Mining District and the burgeoning cattle empires in the Sacramento and Hualapai valleys made the town prominent and an indispensable supply center. As a result, the Arizona Territorial Legislature designated Mineral Park the Mohave County seat in 1877.

Free-roaming burros are a common sight throughout the rocky slopes and canyons of the Cerbat and Black mountains.

An adobe cabin is one of the few remnants of Mineral Park, the former Mohave County seat, and reflects almost a century of abandonment.

By the mid-1880s, Mineral Park was home to more than five hundred residents, including several lawyers, doctors, and a justice of the peace. The town even boasted a weekly newspaper, the *Mohave County Miner*.

With the exhaustion of profitably accessible ore bodies, the mines closed and Mineral Park faded from prominence. The county seat and the paper relocated to Kingman in the 1890s. The newspaper is now the daily *Kingman Daily Miner*. Mineral Park's official end came in 1912 with the closure of the post office.

In the late 1960s, the Duval Mining Company began open pit operations near the town site. Today the pit is operated by Mercator Minerals LTD. As a result, the ghost town of Mineral Park consists of little more than the substantial ruins of the mill, a few scattered buildings, extensive ruins on the hillsides, and a cemetery maintained by the mining company.

## WHEN YOU GO

*Mineral Park Road, a 3-mile paved road that provides access to the town site and current mining operation, is located approximately 16 miles north of Kingman on U.S. Highway 93.*

# CERBAT

Located in a rugged but picturesque west-running canyon in the Cerbat Mountains, the town of Cerbat began as a cluster of prospector's tents in the late 1860s. In spite of extensive deposits of gold, silver, lead, and zinc, the remoteness of the area initially negated any hope of extensive development.

Supplies for the fledgling community came from Yuma via a 250-mile steamboat trip up the Colorado River to Hardyville and then 38 miles overland to Cerbat. The processing of ore in California or Wales required an even lengthier trip.

In spite of its location, Cerbat slowly grew to such a level of prominence that in 1872 work began on a road to link the community with the Mohave-Prescott Toll Road, which was the primary route across the northwest corner of the Arizona Territory at the time. The territorial legislature designated Cerbat as the Mohave County seat.

The bleached tailings from dozens of mines dot the hills and mountains in the narrow canyons that hide the ruins of Cerbat.

Weathered headframes—with the Cerbat Mountains as a backdrop—are among the most tangible relics in Cerbat, the former Mohave County seat.

The haunting ruins of ore chutes and headframes reflect almost a century of mining activity in Cerbat.

A drop in silver prices and the exhaustion of ore bodies resulted in many mine closures and a rapid decline for the community. The county seat relocated to Mineral Park in 1877, but mining in Cerbat continued an ebb and flow for a number of years.

By the summer of 1912, Cerbat's population had dwindled from its peak of several hundred to a mere handful, which prompted the closure of the post office. A large number of the remaining buildings were razed during the downturn with materials being used at other locations.

A ranch at the mouth of the canyon is now the only standing residence in the area. The town site consists of extensive stonewalls and foundations choked by thickets of mesquite and cacti, as well as a wide array of mine-related building shells, head frames, and tailings that span more than a century of activity in the canyon.

## WHEN YOU GO

*Cerbat is located approximately 10 miles northwest of Kingman. The town site is accessed by driving 8 miles north on U.S. Highway 93 to the historic marker that provides a brief history of Cerbat. The final 2 miles begin with a very sandy road that becomes rocky and rutted beyond the ranch. The ranch owners require all visitors sign in before visiting Cerbat.*

# HACKBERRY

Hackberry is one of those towns where fame and prosperity proved to be quite elusive. Considering the history associated with the town site, this is rather surprising.

A spring near the current town site is the one most likely used by the Father Garces expedition of 1775 as it moved east through Truxton Canyon. Lieutenant Amiel W. Whipple visited the same spring in 1854 before he turned south to follow the Big Sandy from its headwaters near Hackberry. In 1857, Lieutenant Edward Fitzgerald Beale surveyed a route that traveled west and named the spring Gardiner.

In 1871, a party of prospectors found a rich vein of gold ore about a mile west of the spring. A large hackberry tree at the site gave the mine and resultant town its name.

The mine proved rich enough to warrant construction of a five stamp mill, and by 1874, the community was showing so much promise that the territorial legislature discussed making the town the county seat. However, within two years, the primary ore body had been exhausted, and the town began a quick fade that ended with the community balanced precariously on the edge of oblivion.

In late 1881, the town's spring again became an important commodity with the arrival of the railroad. The track followed the Beale Wagon Road west of town and crossed northern Arizona into eastern California. Hackberry served as a supply center to the railroad, and local ranches and gave the community a new, tenuous lease on life. Hackberry also met the needs of travelers on the National Old Trails Highway in 1914, and after 1926, Route 66 ensured the little town a modicum of prosperity.

The lapse into obscurity was a lengthy one for Hackberry. It began with Kingman assuming the primary role as supply center for ranching and mining in the area, continued with the conversion to diesel locomotives by the railroad, and culminated with the bypass of Route 66 by Interstate 40. The town settled into a quiet existence for a time with a few local ranching families calling it home.

Today a strip mining operation has broken the silence, and Route 66 fans have given the Hackberry General Store a new lease on life. Other vestiges of the towns' history include a Mission-style, two-room schoolhouse, which was the last operated in the state of Arizona; a scenic cemetery; the towering water tanks that once supplied steam-powered locomotives; and a few old cabins.

The Hackberry General Store, an icon among fans of Route 66, dates to the mid-1930s realignment of the highway.

There is still life in Hackberry that links the modern romanticism of Route 66 with the era of Spanish exploration, as evidenced by the town's tiny post office.

The growing resentment among the Hualapai people with the federal government's policy of sending their children to a boarding school in Fort Mohave on the Colorado River led to the establishment of the Hackberry Day School by the Massachusetts Indian Association in 1894. Many Hualapai lived and worked in the hills around Hackberry, and they defused an increasingly volatile situation even though the entire concept of this school system was offensive to the Native Americans.

During the second year of operation, overseers deemed the school would better serve students and their families with a relocation four miles east to the George Aitken Ranch. Low attendance prevented the school from achieving its primary goal of moving the children from a traditional to conventional lifestyle.

In 1898, President William McKinley issued an executive order creating the Hualapai Indian School Reserve on acreage adjacent to the day school. In 1900, construction began on the Truxton Canyon Training School, and it was created with bricks fired by the students.

By the 1930s, a series of expansions had transformed the school into a vast complex that consisted of a large school, offices, a laundry facility, a detention house, an infirmary, cottages for staff, and a dormitory. There was also a reservoir, a small dairy, and a blacksmith shop.

Many remnants remain to cast long shadows toward Route 66 below. These include the substantial schoolhouse, the office building, and numerous cottages now occupied by Bureau of Indian Affairs employees who work at the Truxton Canyon Agency, which is located on the old school grounds.

## WHEN YOU GO

*From Kingman, drive 21 miles east on Route 66. Park at the Hackberry General Store. The town itself is on the south side of the railroad tracks and is accessed by following Hackberry Road across the sandy Truxton Wash.*

# SIGNAL

Unlike many mining communities on the frontier of the Arizona Territory, the town of Signal blossomed, boomed, and settled into a rather stable existence that spanned decades in spite of extreme isolation.

In late 1874, an amazingly rich silver strike led to the creation of the McCracken Mine and the Owens mining district. Shortly after this, another equally rich strike nearby became the Signal Mine.

In early 1877, Signal began to evolve from a haphazard camp of tents and shacks to a real town that met the needs of those who worked at both mines, the mill, and on area ranches. By October of that year, the population, nearing eight hundred, warranted the establishment of a post office.

Although little differentiated Signal from other dusty mining camps, this community did have one business that set it apart—a brewery. For a brief time, with the exceptions of the mines, this was the most lucrative enterprise in the area.

Extreme isolation was always the community's bane. Merchants initially ordered supplies six months in advance. The inventories were shipped from San Francisco to Yuma, then up the Colorado River by steamboat to Aubrey Landing, and then thirty-five miles by mule team into the mountains along the Big Sandy.

By the mid-1880s, productivity at the area's two principle mines had dramatically declined. The population of the town corresponded with the decline and dwindled to a few hundred.

Sporadic mining fueled a number of small booms and busts, but isolation and profitability of the mine operation became insurmountable problems by the early twentieth century. The final chapter in the town's demise was the discontinuance of the post office in May 1932.

Today, little remains, aside from extensive scattered foundations, mine tailings, assorted discarded equipment, and an isolated ranch house. An additional attraction is the scenic area that surrounds the town site.

The closure of the last two-room school in Arizona marked the end of an era for the state and the town of Hackberry.

Relics from the glory days in Hackberry are quickly vanishing because of the harsh desert climates of western Arizona.

## WHEN YOU GO

*From Wikieup, drive south on U.S. Highway 93 for approximately 8 miles, turn right on to Signal Road, and continue 16 miles. The road is rocky and sandy.*

# GHOSTS OF
# ARIZONA'S
# WEST COAST

THE COLORADO RIVER HAS FOREVER ERASED many of the ghosts of the West Coast. The river, which was the reason for the existence of most villages, has over the years changed course, overflowed its banks, and been harnessed by dams that created lakes that swept over the old town sites.

Housing and commercial development, restricted military access areas, and time have taken their toll on others. The remaining relics from the frontier era, such as the territorial prison at Yuma, are rare gems.

Seeking out survivors can be well worth the effort. Each profiled in this section provides a tangible link to distinct periods that were stepping stones to the modern Southwest.

Temperatures in the deserts and valleys that border the Colorado River in Arizona are often the highest in the nation during the summer months. Exploration is best done during late fall, winter, and early spring.

The desolate cemetery and well-worn trails through the desert are among the last tangible links to the once prosperous river community of Ehrenberg.

The old Cantina in Castle Dome appears to be a portal in the territorial days of old Arizona.

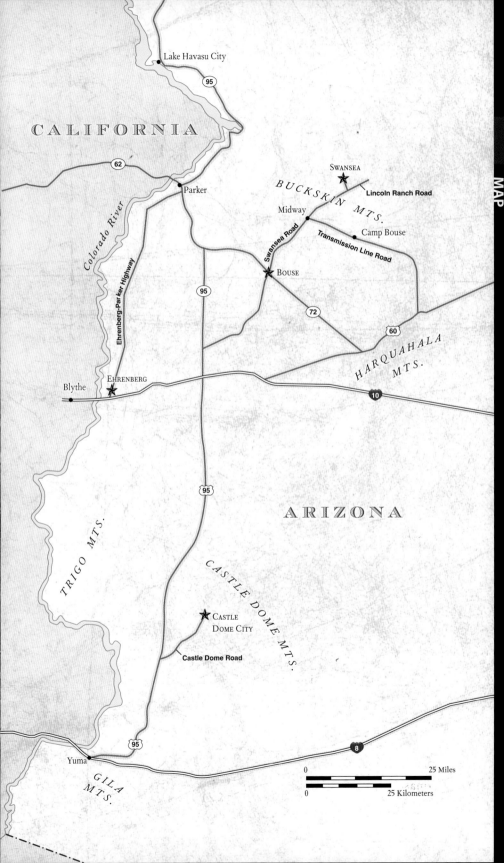

Lake Havasu City

95

CALIFORNIA

62

Parker

95

*Colorado River*

*Ehrenberg-Parker Highway*

SWANSEA

**Lincoln Ranch Road**

BUCKSKIN MTS.

Midway

Camp Bouse

*Swansea Road*

**Transmission Line Road**

BOUSE

72

60

HARQUAHALA MTS.

EHRENBERG

Blythe

10

TRIGO MTS.

95

ARIZONA

CASTLE DOME MTS.

CASTLE DOME CITY

**Castle Dome Road**

95

8

Yuma

GILA MTS.

0                    25 Miles

0                    25 Kilometers

# EHRENBERG

The capricious Colorado River was a key component in the early development of the Arizona Territory. Before the development of the railroad, steamboats and river ports served as primary modes of transportation to supply the remote mining camps and military outposts scattered throughout the deserts and mountains.

A discovery of gold placers along the Colorado River in 1862 led to the establishment of La Paz. A year later, a group of investors hired Herman Ehrenberg to survey a town site six miles downriver from La Paz. The town of Ehrenberg, which was initially established as Mineral City, languished in the shadow of its more prosperous neighbor. Martha Summerhayes, a young bride traveling up the Colorado River by steamer noted, "One morning, as I was trying to finish out a nap in my stateroom, Jack came excitedly in and said, 'Get up Martha, we are coming to Ehrenberg!' Visions of castles on the Rhine and stories of the Middle Ages floated through my mind, as I sprang up, in pleasurable anticipation of seeing an interesting and beautiful place. Alas for my ignorance. I saw but a row of low thatched hovels, perched on the edge of the ragged looking river bank; a road ran lengthwise along, and opposite the hovels I saw a store and some more mean looking huts of adobe . . ."

By 1869, Ehrenberg had grown to a size that warranted the establishment of a post office, but it was still a ragged frontier community in comparison to La Paz, the Yuma County seat. Within twenty-four months, the roles reversed as a result of exhausted gold placer fields and the Colorado River changing its course.

By 1875, La Paz had withered to such a point the post office was discontinued, while the population of Ehrenberg had grown to more than five hundred. Among the businesses relocated from La Paz was the store owned by Joseph and Mike Goldwater, the latter was the grandfather of Barry Goldwater.

Most frontier communities had at least one character who was colorful enough to stand out in a sea of characters. In Ehrenberg, it was Jesus Daniel, the one-armed postmaster whose obsession for prospecting left little time for his duties. When the post office inspector arrived unexpectedly, he found more than 150 undelivered letters, including a commendation for Daniel's efficiency from the postmaster general.

Weathered headboards and fresh offerings hint that for one family, this Ehrenberg pioneer is gone but not forgotten.

Piles of stone where cacti struggle to survive in the Ehrenberg cemetery show how forbidding and hostile this land can be.

Ehrenberg enjoyed steady growth through the remaining years of the nineteenth century until the railroad surpassed the river as a primary conduit for commerce in the Arizona Territory. The community entered a period of rapid decline after 1900, and the post office closed on December 31, 1913.

The creation of a trailer park in the mid-1950s erased many surviving structures from the frontier era. The cemetery, located about a half-mile north of present-day Ehrenberg, features a monument erected by the Arizona State Highway Department in 1935, and other remnants offer the most tangible connections to this historic community.

## WHEN YOU GO

*Ehrenberg is located along Interstate 10. From Blythe, California, take exit 1 after crossing the Colorado River.*

# SWANSEA

The history of the Southwest's frontier era is confusing—with many twists, turns, and contradictory documentation. The story of Swansea is a perfect example.

Sketchy information indicates prospectors were working rich deposits of silver in the area of the Buckskin Mountains as early as 1862. As the processing of the ore required transport to the Colorado River thirty miles to the east, shipping downriver to the Gulf of Mexico at Yuma, and then across the Atlantic to Wales, only the purest and most profitable ores were extracted.

Although the community in Wales was the inspiration for this desert community's name, it was not the result of this association. George Mitchell, a metallurgist for the Consolidated Gold and Copper Mining Company who hailed from Swansea, bestowed the name.

Prospecting and mining continued sporadically until 1886 when the profitable silver bodies were exhausted. The prospectors moved on to new finds and left behind vast deposits of copper, a mineral not profitable enough to work in such a remote location.

In 1904, the Signal Group purchased a large number of the old mining claims and planned to develop them for the copper reserves. There were even plans for a small community, Signal, to be built on site.

Rusting remnants preserved in a state of suspended decay make Swansea unique among the ghosts of the Southwest.

*Above:* Vestiges from a time when the streets of Swansea teemed with activity, and the town even supported an automobile dealership are scattered among the desert brush.

*Opposite:* Preservation efforts in Swansea include keeping roofs on the remaining structures to ensure future generations can experience the haunting beauty of a desert ghost town.

As was so often the case, the company lacked adequate capital for such an endeavor and began to search began for investors in 1906. Enter George Mitchell who made the twenty-one-mile trip from Bouse, the closest town with a railroad, with T. J. Carrigan of Consolidated Gold and Copper Mining Company.

The arduous journey was a failure for the Signal Group because the new investors decided to purchase the claims outright rather than partner for development. However, the trip was a resounding success for Mitchell, who was awarded a lucrative position with the new company.

By the early spring of 1909, the new mining camp had a large enough population to warrant a post office. Through the following decade, the fortunes of the mines fluctuated with the price of copper, but the town continued to grow.

Swansea's era of isolation ended with completion of a spur line from Bouse. Its residents enjoyed a wide array of amenities, including a theater, a realty company, several general merchandise stores, a barber, a physician, saloons, restaurants, an automobile dealership, and a newspaper, *Swansea Times*, published by Angela Hammer.

After the Consolidated Gold and Copper Mining Company went bankrupt in 1912, various other companies worked the mine and operated the mill until 1922. The town began a rapid slide into abandonment with the closure of the mines.

Today Swansea is a true ghost town with a population of zero. However, unlike most ghost towns in the Southwest, the Bureau of Land Management maintains the remnants of the community in an arrested state of decay that provides visitors with a truly unique opportunity.

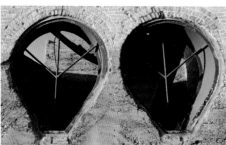

*Above:* Towering mounds of melting adobe on the desolate desert plain infuse Swansea with a forlorn sense of emptiness.

*Left:* The substantial ruins of the mill in Swansea produce unusual blends of shadows and color in the desert sun.

## WHEN YOU GO

*From Bouse, follow Main Street to Rayder Avenue, which will turn into Swansea Road, and turn left. Bear left at the first fork in the road shortly after leaving Bouse. Three landmarks ensure you are on the right road: the crossing of the Central Arizona Project Canal; the interpretive kiosk at Midway, a former water stop for the railroad spur from Bouse to Swansea; and a four-way stop where you will turn left. The road is sandy and rocky. Four-wheel drive is not a necessity, but ground clearance is a definite must. Fall, winter, and early spring are the best months to visit.*

51

# BOUSE

Mining in the mountains around Bouse began in the early 1860s but was sporadic until the arrival of the railroad shortly after the turn of the century. The railroad also sparked the establishment of a company store, the Brayton Commercial Company, to meet the needs of employees at the Harquahala Mine. There was also agricultural development in the area because ground water was plentiful.

In an odd turn of events, when the application for a post office was filed in 1907, the postal department approved the request under the name Thomas Bouse, the primary applicant's name, rather than Brayton, which was on the original application.

A spur line to Swansea, the development of other mines in the area, and farming fueled the slow but steady growth of Bouse well into the 1920s. After the profitable ore bodies were exhausted and the Great Depression, the quiet desert's population froze at less than two hundred.

Then, in late 1941, a historical event on the other side of the world gave the old mining town a new lease on life. Shortly after the attack on Pearl Harbor, the U.S. Army began seeking suitable locations to train troops for the invasion of North Africa.

The thirty-five million–acre Desert Training Center and California-Arizona Maneuver Area, created under guidance from General George S. Patton Jr., was carved from the heart of the desert Southwest as the world's largest military training facility. Numerous camps and specialty training centers were scattered throughout this vast military reservation.

The need for secrecy was paramount for testing equipment that represented the cutting edge of military technology. Few places were as remote as the Butler Valley twenty miles north of Bouse. It was here that Camp Bouse, the Area 51 of its day, was established to test the revolutionary Canal Defense Light, a tank defense system.

Bouse became a boomtown long before the first troops arrived in August 1943. It was, however, a short-lived boom as the camp soon closed, and in April 1944, the buildings and a great deal of surplus equipment were sold.

Agriculture and retirees who come to enjoy the mild winter temperatures are now the lifeblood of this small community. Vestiges of its historic past abound and include the assay office, which is now a museum, and a monument that includes a World War II tank at the intersection of State Highway 72 and Plamosa Road.

## WHEN YOU GO

*From Parker, drive south 12 miles on U.S. Highway 95. At the junction of U.S. 95 and State Highway 72, continue on Highway 72 for 14 miles. To reach Camp Bouse, drive northeast on Main Street in Bouse. At the stop sign, turn left on Rayder Drive, which turns into Swansea Road. Go 2.2 miles to the Bouse "Y" trailhead, which is marked by the Bureau of Land Management information sign on the left. Take the left fork and continue on Swansea Road and turn right on Transmission Line Road. Camp Bouse is 25 miles from Bouse. There are long stretches of deep sand on the road.*

# CASTLE DOME CITY

The history of Castle Dome City is a lengthy tale. When American prospectors first arrived in the area of what would become Castle Dome City in 1858, they found weathered excavations and old mine dumps shadowed by mature Palo Verde and ironwood trees that may have been more than a century old.

The first major discoveries of galena (a silver and lead mix) ore happened in 1863, but extensive development of the area was delayed because of the Civil

War. However, by 1870, the district was booming, and its center was this raucous mining camp.

Initially the ore was hand sorted, sacked, and hauled overland to Castle Dome Landing on the Colorado River, where it was shipped by riverboat to the

Castle Dome is far more than a ghost town. It is a dusty time capsule that has preserved a glimpse of life on the Arizona Territory frontier.

An attention to detail in the preservation and resurrection of Castle Dome is evident throughout this historic frontier-era community.

Visiting Castle Dome is like stepping into another time, when Doc Holliday haunted the faro tables and Wyatt Earp walked the dusty streets.

Gulf of California and then by schooner to San Francisco for smelting. The cost of production dropped dramatically with the opening of a smelter in Yuma in 1875 and even further when the Southern Pacific Railroad arrived in Yuma in 1876.

By the last decades of the nineteenth century, the rough-and-tumble mining camp was one of the largest in southwestern Arizona. Shady, nefarious,

Many of the vintage props that transform Castle Dome into a three-dimensional portrait of life on the frontier were recovered from area dumps.

hopeful, and opportunistic people from throughout the world flooded into the area. Legend has it that many icons of western history, such as Doc Holliday and Wyatt Earp, walked these dusty streets and tried their luck at the faro tables.

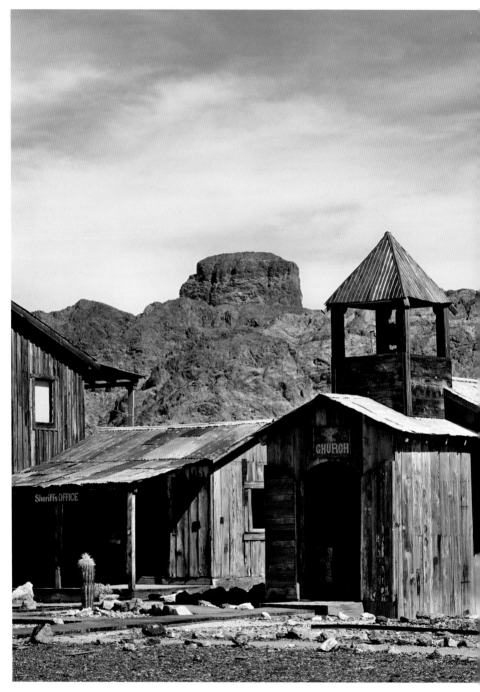

With the Castle Dome Mountains as backdrop, Castle Dome seems to look more like a movie set than a ghost town.

The population fluctuated with the fortunes of the mines that produced copious amounts of lead, which kept the town alive throughout the Great Depression and during both world wars. At its peak in 1915, the town was large enough to support a modern hotel, a theater, a dress shop, several mercantile stores, numerous saloons, a garage, a gas station, a brothel, and a church with stained glass windows.

By 1947, declining markets, the cost to update the mining properties, and other factors sent the town into a rapid and steep downfall. In 1948, the population had dropped to the point where the school and most businesses closed.

A few hardy souls still hung on and managed to eke out a living from processing the ore dumps and expanding the drifts and tunnels of the old mines. This continued well into the early 1990s.

A new chapter for the old camp began in 1993, when Allen Armstrong and his wife, Stephanie, purchased the twenty-six-acre town site nestled against the picturesque Kofa National Wildlife Refuge. At that time, the town consisted of twenty broken-down buildings, extensive ruins, and acres of refuse from more than a century of mining.

Today the entire town has become a museum of sorts with the remaining buildings restored to various degrees—from how they were when the town thrived to how they looked shortly after abandonment. A wide array of artifacts is on display in a museum and around the town and range from a pair of Levi's from the 1890s, which is possibly the world's oldest pair, to Spanish Colonial–era boot covers.

## WHEN YOU GO

*From Yuma, drive north on U.S. Highway 95 to mile marker 55 and turn right onto Castle Dome Road. Proceed 10 miles, and turn left at the intersection and continue for about 2 miles. Four-wheel drive is not a necessity, but ground clearance is recommended. Late fall, winter, and spring are the best times to visit. Castle Dome Museum is open every day except Monday. Admission is $5 for adults and $2 for children.*

# GHOSTS OF SOUTHERN ARIZONA

SANTA CRUZ COUNTY IS ONE OF THE SMALLEST IN ARIZONA. It is also one of the most historic.

In January 1691, Father Eusebio Francisco Kino visited the village of Guevavi, which is a few miles north of present-day Nogales. In 1736, a great silver discovery near Arisoona sparked a rush of adventurers from all the Spanish colonies and throughout Europe, which in turn led to the establishment of a presidio at Tubac in 1752.

Santa Cruz County, with Tubac as the centerpiece, may be the cradle of Arizona history, but for the Old West enthusiast, Cochise County is the Holy Grail and Shangri-La all rolled into one. Here lie Bisbee, Tombstone, Wilcox, Charleston, Fort Bowie on the old Butterfield Stage Road, the Chiricahua Mountains, the stronghold of Cochise, and a monument to the surrender of Geronimo.

However, not all of the old towns found here are dry bones. One town still offers fine dining and lodging in rooms once occupied by legends such as Theodore Roosevelt and John Wayne.

Beautiful desert wildflowers provide a colorful contrast to the melting adobe walls, ruins, and austere landscapes of Ruby.

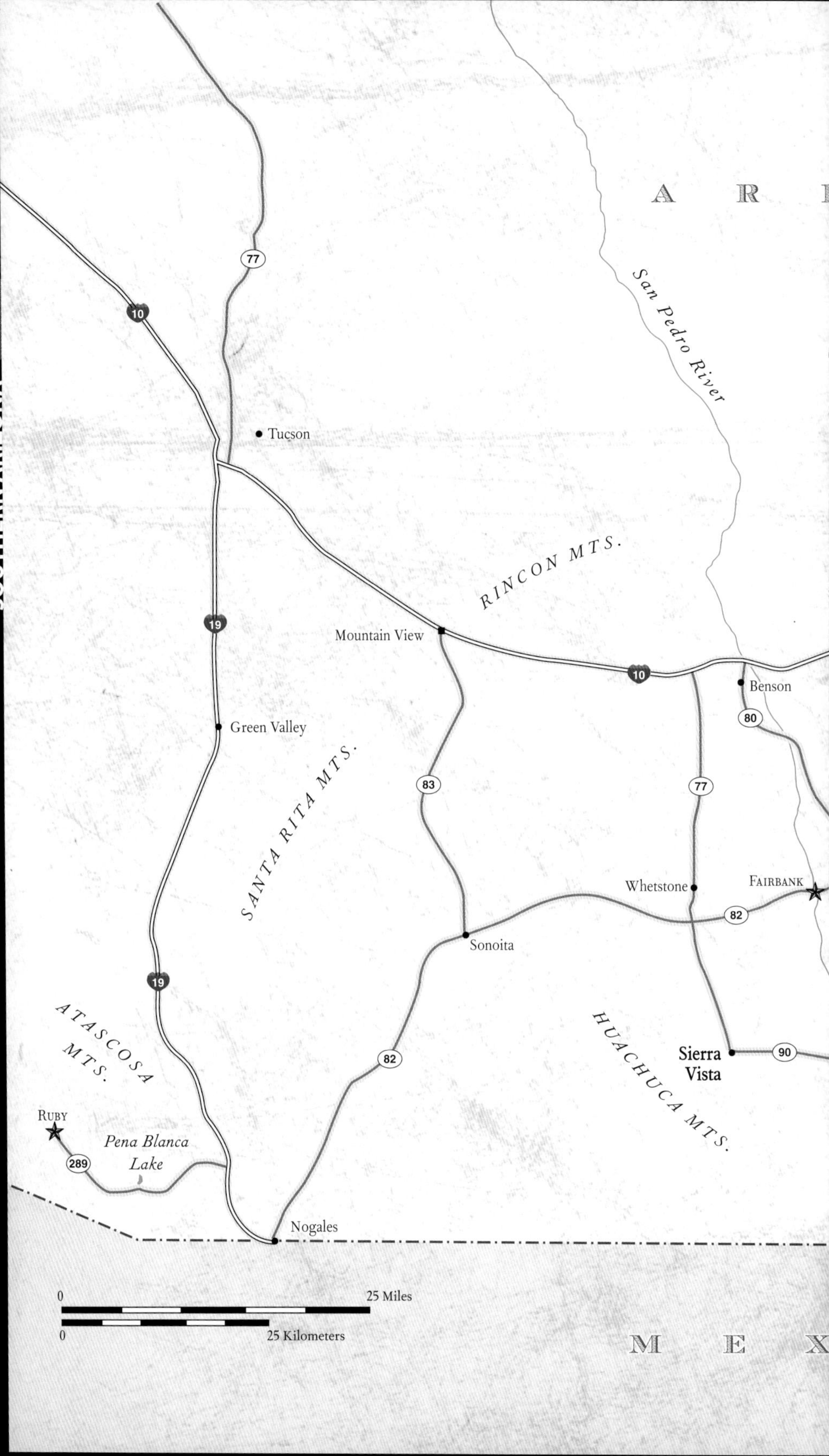

A R

San Pedro River

(77)

(10)

● Tucson

(19)

RINCON MTS.

Mountain View ●

(10)

● Benson

(80)

● Green Valley

SANTA RITA MTS.

(83)

(77)

Whetstone ●      FAIRBANK ★

(82)

Sonoita ●

ATASCOSA
MTS.

(19)

HUACHUCA MTS.

(82)

Sierra
Vista ●      (90)

RUBY
★

Pena Blanca
Lake

(289)

Nogales ●

0                                      25 Miles

0                          25 Kilometers

M      E      X

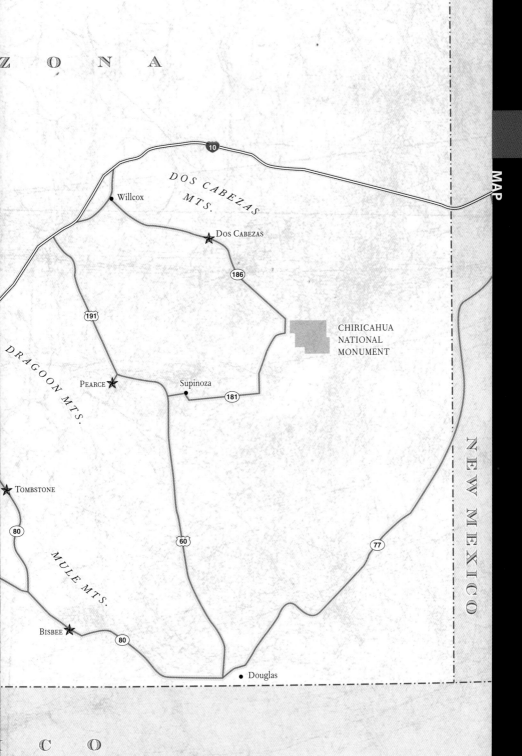

Z O N A

DOS CABEZAS MTS.

Willcox

DOS CABEZAS

10

186

191

DRAGOON MTS.

PEARCE

Supinoza

181

CHIRICAHUA
NATIONAL
MONUMENT

NEW MEXICO

TOMBSTONE

80

60

77

MULE MTS.

BISBEE

80

Douglas

C O

# RUBY

Extracting the deposits of silver ore found in the shadow of Montana Peak dates to the mid-eighteenth century. However, a full century passed before work began in earnest after Herman Ehrenberg and Charles Poston discovered a rich ore body in 1854.

For more than thirty years, miners and prospectors worked their claims and were continuously lured on by new discoveries that always seemed to be one step away from the mother lode. The little community established to meet the miners' needs reflected the hardscrabble life of the men and was little more than a ragged collection of shacks and tents known as Montana Camp.

The mercantile was established in 1888, and the big strike finally came three years later and the boom was on. As a testimony of the camp's promising future, Julius Andrews, the owner of the mercantile, made an application for a post office and named the community Ruby in homage to his wife, Lillie B. Ruby, in 1909.

The town prospered with the expansion of the mines. At its peak, the primary mine employed three hundred men. The school's enrollment was almost 150 students during the same time period. In 1941, the Eagle Pitcher Company, operator of the mine, suspended operations. The town was a true ghost with a population of zero within five years.

Tragically, a series of brutal murders gave Ruby notoriety rather than silver or gold. The camp's remote location and proximity to the Mexican border, less than twenty miles away, made the area a haven for bandits and parties of renegade Native Americans.

In February 1920, a Mexican ranch hand stopped at the store and found Alex and John Frazier, two brothers who were the storekeeper and postmaster, shot dead. The safe was open and empty, and the town's only phone was ripped from the wall. Months of investigation failed to identify the murderer or murderers.

In August 1921, the store was robbed again and its new owners, Frank and Myrtle Pearson, were killed, and Elizabeth Purcell, a sister-in-law, was wounded. The local area was stirred to vigilante levels because the robbers used their gun to remove Myrtle's five gold teeth as she lay dying.

The recession after World War I and the collapse of cotton prices in the 1920s initiated a decline that followed almost a century of growth in Arizona. A twenty-five percent decrease in the demand for copper in 1929—fueled by the Great Depression—escalated the drop.

The population of the state declined by fifty thousand people between 1932 and 1936, which was due largely to an exodus of residents from mining towns. Nearly every copper mine in the state either closed or drastically curtailed its production. Many communities that were established when Arizona was still a territory became ghost towns. A few clung to life and were inhabited by a few hardy residents who scratched a subsistence living from placer mining or reworking old mine dumps.

The resurgent interest in placer mining during the Great Depression led to the establishment of small hardscrabble camps and the rediscovery of once-forgotten frontier communities.

An abundance of water made Ruby unique among Arizona mining camps. Today, it is an oasis for Arizona ghost town hunters.

Empty windows and broken walls frame scenes of stunning desert landscapes under breathtaking skies throughout Ruby.

A posse set out to look for the outlaws, and for the first time in Arizona history, an airplane aided in the search to track the bandits. The trail was lost at the Mexican border, but in April 1922, a bartender in Sonora notified authorities about a man trying to sell gold teeth. Manuel Martinez and Placido Silvas were arrested and quickly extradited to Arizona.

The scattered remnants of everyday life in Ruby have a haunting, surreal air that suggests the town is suspended between abandonment and collapse.

After a short trial, Martinez received the death penalty and Silvas was sentenced to life in prison, but during transport to the state prison at Florence, they overpowered two deputies and caused the car to overturn. The outlaws' newfound freedom lasted six days, and on August 10, 1923, the execution of Martinez proceeded on schedule.

A vintage truck silently guards the ghostly secrets and colorful history of Ruby.

Today, Ruby is preserved thanks to the Arizona State Parks. A heritage grant allows for a caretaker and limited maintenance of structures. This state of preservation, as well as the beautiful mountain scenery, makes a trip to Ruby one not quickly forgotten.

## WHEN YOU GO

*From Nogales, drive north on Interstate 19 for 21 miles to State Highway 289 and turn west. Follow the signs and continue west 25 miles. Four-wheel drive is not needed, but ground clearance is important.*

# DOS CABEZAS

Dos Cabezas is Spanish for two heads, which is a description of the mountains near the town. For centuries, these distinctive rocky knobs were a welcome sight to travelers because a spring that supplies fresh water year-round is only a half mile from the town of Dos Cabezas. The life-giving waters became a point of contention between the Apaches and Spanish conquistadors who began to explore the area in the late sixteenth century. The battle for control of this vital resource continued for more than three hundred years.

In 1851, an American boundary survey party mapped a route through Apache Pass, which was another important source for dependable water several miles to the south of Dos Cabezas. The surveyors noted both springs and named the springs in the shadow of the Dos Cabezas knobs Elwell Springs. This water source was vital to travelers on the Southern Overland Trail headed to California.

Thick brush, mesquite, and Palo Verde trees engulf the desolate adobe ruins in Dos Cabezas and hide the faint traces of others.

In 1858, rich ore bodies were discovered at the present site of Dos Cabezas and sparked a small flood of adventurers willing to risk the near-constant threat of attack by Apaches, who were intent on repelling the invaders. John Butterfield needed the security of the fledgling mining camp and the dependable waters of the springs, so he established his stage station halfway between Elwell Springs and Dos Cabezas.

By 1860, the station had become an important stop for prospectors, travelers on the Butterfield stage line, and as a refuge against warring Apache bands. Within twenty years, the nearby mining camp had become a town with a population of three hundred residents that supported a hotel, a blacksmith shop, several saloons, and a stamp mill for processing ore.

A few hardy souls still call the historic community of Dos Cabezas home and ranch along the old Butterfield Overland Stage Road in the shadow of the town's namesake peak.

With the discovery of rich copper deposits in 1906, the boom that had begun more than forty years previously went into high gear. The Mascot Copper Company, Inc. was organized to develop the discovery. It brought in the most modern equipment, built an office complex, mill, power station, dormitories, theater, and cafeteria. A spur line connected Dos Cabezas from the main rail line at Wilcox, fourteen miles to the northwest.

For twenty years, new discoveries and outstanding profits made the Mascot Copper Company a regular feature in mining journals. However, the copper deposits were exhausted with startling abruptness, three hundred employees received their final checks, and the company began to demolish most of the company structures.

The town held on through the Great Depression with a few residents scratching out a living by working claims in the surrounding mountains or ranching. Dos Cabezas experienced a brief resurgence during World War II when there was a renewed interest in the old mines, but it continued its slide during the 1950s. The post office, which first opened in 1879, closed its doors on January 31, 1960.

The business district in Dos Cabezas consists of brush-choked ruins, the post office that closed in 1960, and the faint outline of foundations.

The old town is less than a shadow of what it once was, but a few who treasure solitude still call it home. The extensive ruins and picturesque backdrop provide photographers with endless possibilities.

By 1915, the postmark date on this card, the Mascot Copper Company was on its way to becoming the largest copper producer in Arizona. *Author collection*

## WHEN YOU GO

*From Willcox, drive 28 miles south on State Highway 186.*

# PEARCE

Jimmie Pearce and his wife were hardworking, frugal folks who dreamed of owning a ranch. After working at mines in a number of camps, they arrived in Tombstone during its boom. Jimmie worked in the mines, and his wife worked in a boarding house. Both ventures proved lucrative, and soon they had saved enough for their ranch.

With their sons who longed to be cowboys, the Pearces purchased a spread in the wide Sulphur Springs Valley in the shadow of the Dragoon Mountains. Legend has it that in 1894, Jimmie was resting on a hilltop, surveying his corner of paradise, when a piece of quartz caught his miner-trained eye. Jimmie was literally sitting on a gold mine. He named his new find the Commonwealth and staked out five claims, one for each member of the family.

For a while, the mine was a family affair, although the enterprise attracted numerous offers from eager buyers. John Brockman, a banker from Silver City, New Mexico, finally persuaded Jimmie to sell the mine for the sum of $250,000

The looming clouds of a summer storm and deep blue desert skies serve as a backdrop for the haunting emptiness of downtown Pearce, Arizona.

As seen from the front porch of the Pearce general store/museum to the distant horizon, little indicates that this was once a prosperous and bustling town.

The Pearce post office opened its doors in March 1896, but a diminishing population since the 1930s makes its continued existence tenuous at best.

The general store in Pearce is one of the last remnants from a business district that once included a theater, several stores, saloons, restaurants, and a garage.

and agreed that Jimmie's wife would have exclusive rights to operate the only boarding house at the mine.

The town of Pearce appeared on the valley floor below the mine almost overnight. Because Tombstone was in decline, a few businessmen there dismantled their businesses and shipped them over the Dragoon Mountains to take advantage of the new opportunities. Another Pearce legend is that the first rooming house was built of lumber from the Tombstone jail.

By 1919, a rail line from Wilcox linked Pearce to the outside world, and the business district boasted a theater and several restaurants, saloons, hotels, and garages. The community also supported a school, mill, and several churches.

The hard times of the Great Depression and the decline of profitable and accessible ores led to the mine's closure in the early 1930s. Pearce was a ghost town within weeks of the mine's closure.

Today the town's business district consists of a combination general store and museum that is randomly open and a post office. The remainder of the town consists of a wide array of ruins and scattered relics.

## WHEN YOU GO

*From Wilcox, drive 28 miles south on U.S. Highway 191. Pearce is about a half mile off the highway on a well-marked road.*

# BISBEE

The Mule Mountains, located fifteen miles south of Tombstone, are a relatively small but rugged range running about thirty miles in length from north to south and fifteen miles wide. The craggy canyons and numerous springs made them a veritable fortress for the Apaches who launched raids into the Sulphur Springs Valley and the San Pedro Valley.

A steep-sided canyon pass filled with numerous springs and seeps is located at the southern end of the mountains. Mexican traders named the canyon Puerto de las Mulas, which translates to Mule Pass. In 1877, Jack Dunn, a government tracker, was trailing an Apache war party through this canyon with the Sixth Cavalry, Company C, when he stumbled upon a rocky ledge with a wide quartz vein laced with gold. Developing the claim was not a priority or feasible for Dunn because the area was essentially a war zone at the time.

Fast forward to 1880. Opportunists from throughout the world come to the area due to word of mouth, the company mining Dunn's find expands at an astounding rate, and a town quickly spreads into the surrounding canyons.

By 1881, the Copper Queen Mine was running twenty-four hours a day and was one of the most productive mines in the country. Enter Dr. James Douglas,

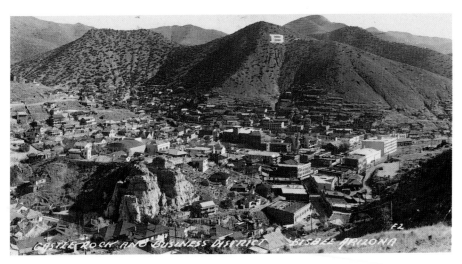

The view of Bisbee and its surrounding mountains hasn't changed much since 1946, which is the postmark date on this card. *Author collection*

a world famous geologist and metallurgist who was commissioned by a group of eastern speculators to evaluate properties at Jerome and throughout Arizona. He was so impressed with what he found in the Mule Mountains that he convinced the speculators, owners of Phelps Dodge, an import/export business, to expand into mining.

Bisbee was named after Judge DeWitt Bisbee, a principal financial backer of the mine. The town that sprang up around the Copper Queen was a typical rowdy mining camp. Oddly, the town's namesake never visited the canyon-bound community.

By the late 1880s, Bisbee was well on the way to becoming a modern city with two distinct districts. Tombstone Canyon became the main thoroughfare, and Brewery Gulch was in an intersecting canyon and known as the shady side of town. Al Sieber, legendary scout for General George Crook during the Apache campaigns, opened the first business in the gulch when he dug a hole in the side of the canyon and established a brewery; hence, the canyon's name.

The demand for copper during World War I sent the mineral's price and company profits soaring. Union leaders underestimated the far-reaching power of the mining companies and the overall mood of most mining camps when they decided this was an opportune time to strike for better wages.

The Industrial Workers of the World led the assault on the mining companies. Phelps Dodge–controlled newspapers responded with scathing editorials on the unions.

At 6:30 a.m. on July 12, 1917, the feud boiled over into violence on the streets of Bisbee. An estimated two thousand armed men accosted an estimated two thousand union members and their sympathizers and herded them into the Warren baseball park. More than one thousand people were loaded into boxcars for a one-way trip to Columbus, New Mexico. Amazingly, there were only two deaths on that day, which is now known as the infamous Bisbee Deportation.

By the turn of the century, Bisbee was a substantial community built of cut stone and brick with a reputation for being a cultured, modern city with the latest amenities and marvels. Residents enjoyed the luxury of electricity, phone service, a streetcar line, and even a stock exchange. The town was still a mining camp and not immune from violence. The worst crime in the city's history took place the week before Christmas in 1883.

Five men rode into town and held up the Goldwater-Casteneda store. During the robbery, the man left outside with the horses panicked and opened fire on a man he thought had a gun. When the smoke cleared, five citizens were dead, including a pregnant woman.

After a lengthy manhunt, all five were captured. A sixth man, John Heith, who owned a dance hall in Bisbee, was the mastermind behind the robbery and implicated. The five robbers received a death sentence while Heith received a lighter sentence. He was to serve at the Territorial Prison at Yuma for robbery. The area

Long afternoon shadows cloak this venerable mining camp that bridges the past and present with seamless beauty.

residents were so outraged they stormed the Cochise County Jail in Tombstone and hung Heith from a telegraph pole on Tough Nut Street. This was the only vigilante hanging in Tombstone's history.

With the closure of the mines in 1974, the queen of the mining camps became a frontier-era time capsule as a quiet village nestled in gorgeous scenery. The narrow canyons squeezed Bisbee into a series of terraces cut into the canyon walls, which made it a treasure box of unique historic architecture and a photographer's paradise.

The prosperity derived from being the county seat and one of the world's richest mineral sites is still evident throughout Bisbee—from the stately Copper Queen Hotel, built in 1902, and the old stock exchange, which is now a bar, to the museum in the Copper Queen Mining offices built in 1897 and the Victorian-styled houses and miner's cabins that appear to march up the steep canyon sides.

Bisbee is not a true ghost town in the sense that more than five thousand people still call it home, but its current population is a far cry from its peak of twenty thousand residents. But for the ghost town hunter or fan of western history, Bisbee should be on the top-ten list of must-see places in Arizona. Few things attest to how special Bisbee is more than *Travel and Leisure* magazine naming it one of the Best New American Destinations.

In late 1901, miners working for the Calumet and Arizona Mining Company hit a body of high grade ore that eventually became the richest mine in the world. In the 1930s, the Phelps Dodge Corporation bought the Calumet and Arizona Mining Company and became the literal king of the hill in Bisbee.

Both companies had initiated major open pit mining operations during World War I. The Lavender Pit began with the initial discovery in 1901, and by the time it closed in 1974, it was 900 feet in depth—one of the deepest pit mines in the world.

The mines of the Bisbee area hold another record as the richest mineralized site in the world. When large-scale mining operations ceased in 1975, these mines had produced almost 3 million ounces of gold, more than 97 million ounces of silver, over 8 billion pounds of copper, 340 million pounds of lead, and almost 373 million pounds of zinc.

From near the mouth of the Mule Pass Tunnel, Bisbee appears suspended in time with only traffic to break the illusion.

## WHEN YOU GO

*Bisbee is located 25 miles northwest of Douglas on State Highway 80.*

# TOMBSTONE

Tombstone is a larger-than-life legend built on one shootout near the OK Corral in the fall of 1881. A fascinating and colorful history is lost in the shadow of this event.

Ed Schieffelin had been a prospector since his teenage years, when he searched for riches in Oregon with his father. By the time he arrived in the Arizona territory during the mid-1870s, he was well seasoned and quite capable of reading formations.

Legend is that when he informed his traveling companions, a cavalry troop riding for Fort Huachuca from California, that he planned to explore the San Pedro Valley, which was the very heart of the Apache defenses, they told him that all he would find was his tombstone. When Schieffelin staked two claims near the

San Pedro River on the richest silver deposits found in the territory at the time, he named them Tombstone and Graveyard.

Watervale became the moniker for the mining camp built around Graveyard, but the mine proved to be a pocket rather than a vein. Schieffelin was not concerned about the setback as he had discovered an even richer deposit nearby. The camp residents soon relocated to the new find that became the legendary Toughnut Mine.

Tombstone's historic district blends authentic historic re-creation and movie-set romanticism built on the legend of the OK Corral. The Bird Cage Theater dates to 1881 and initially served as a saloon, burlesque theater, brothel, and dance hall.

The historic Boot Hill cemetery in Tombstone is famous for its headstones with quirky epitaphs set against cinematic western backgrounds.

The first cabin in Tombstone was built in April 1879. The town was incorporated by 1881. By the end of 1882, the town boasted five churches, a school with 250 students, two banks, a newspaper, and 150 establishments licensed to dispense alcohol.

Fire swept through the town in June 1881 and in May 1882 and left little more than smoking ruins. The community continued to grow and prosper until the population neared ten thousand.

Wyatt Earp, Doc Holliday, and Johnny Ringo are the names most often associated with Tombstone. Few realize the community was home to a surprising number of individuals who carved a niche in history but lived lives of relative obscurity.

Doctor George Goodfellow became world famous as the gunshot doctor, an indication of Tombstone's wildness. His work and published papers on the topic contributed greatly to advances in trauma treatment. He was also the first doctor to arrive in Sonora, Mexico, after the great earthquake of 1887. Mexican President Porfirio Diaz awarded him a special medal for his efforts.

A modern hero who hails from Tombstone is Colonel James Macia Jr. During World War II, he was a young, fearless lieutenant who volunteered for a mission with a group now known as Doolittle's Raiders.

Real, as well as re-created, headstones with colorful epitaphs have made the cemetery in Tombstone almost as popular an attraction as the OK Corral.

Tombstone's glory days were surprisingly quite short in number. In 1886, fires destroyed the pumps at the Contention and Grand Central mines and caused them to flood. The Panic of 1893, a tumultuous economic event that included the collapse of silver prices, was another blow.

Efforts to reopen the flooded mines began in 1901, but the pumps failed in 1909. In 1914, Phelps Dodge purchased most of the mining equipment at a receiver's sale. By 1929, Tombstone was well on its way to being a ghost town when Bisbee became the county seat.

Today, Tombstone consists of numerous historic buildings with an overlay of modern, tourist-orientated reconstruction, including the wooden board sidewalks in the historic district.

When my wife's father returned for a family reunion after an absence of many years, he was surprised to find wooden sidewalks had replaced the concrete ones he knew as a child. He was born in Tombstone, and a photo of his grandfather, Joe Hood, the Cochise County sheriff for several years, hangs in the original 1882 courthouse, which is Arizona's smallest state park.

In spite of what the signage that welcomes visitors to Tombstone may indicate, the town was relatively peaceful, at least in comparison to other frontier-era mining towns.

The *Tombstone Epitaph* is one of the oldest newspapers in the state of Arizona and dates to 1881.

Small crosses planted among piles of stone that reflect the frontier era in countless mining camps are scattered among the fanciful headstones in the Tombstone cemetery.

Tombstone's attempt to re-create the frontier era and capitalize on tourism has resulted in the replacement of cement sidewalks with boardwalks in its historic district.

The twentieth century had the Great Depression. The nineteenth century had the Panic of '93. Policies created for political power fueled the depression of the 1890s. In a complicated series of political compromises and backroom deals, the Sherman Silver Purchase Act, sponsored by Senator John Sherman of Ohio, became law on July 14, 1890. It was a measure to restore international confidence in the financial stability of the United States.

There were two key provisions to the bill. One gave authority to the Treasury Department to purchase 4.5 million ounces of silver each month at market rates. The second provision authorized the Treasury Department to issue notes redeemable in gold or silver.

The government purchases amounted to almost the monthly total output from the nation's mines. Without the ability to control the price of silver through the increase or decrease of production, the price of silver plummeted and flooded the market.

Many mine operators suspended operations. Others attempted to stay in business by reducing expenses and cutting the miners' wages, which led to extensive labor problems and sporadic violence. In mere weeks, entire mining communities became ghost towns.

## WHEN YOU GO

*From Bisbee, drive north for 19 miles on State Highway 80.*

# FAIRBANK

Fairbank—named for N. K. Fairbank, a Chicago merchant and primary investor in the Grand Central Mining Company in Tombstone—is one of those special places where the mists of time have obscured a rich and colorful past. Spanish explorers discovered the Native American village on the banks of the San Pedro River in 1692. Its location near a dependable supply of fresh water and lush grass made it an important stop for stages running between Tucson and Tombstone. The arrival

of the railroad in 1881 added to the community's importance because it was a primary stop on the rail line connecting Guaymas, Mexico, with Benson, which made it a key staging area for passenger and freight companies that served the area.

The ruins of Fairbank are the centerpiece for the San Pedro Riparian National Conservation Area and thus are spared further degradation by vandals.

*Above and opposite:* Fairbank's forgotten cemetery is marked by weathered crosses and piles of stone and stands in contrast to the well-preserved, frequently trafficked one in nearby Tombstone.

By 1900, almost twenty years after its initial settlement, the town had a population of nearly one hundred, a Wells Fargo office, a meat market, a general store, several saloons, and a steam-powered mill. With the exception of occasional floods, life in Fairbank was relatively quiet until February of that year.

Bill Stiles and Bert Alvord were Cochise County deputies and also leaders of an outlaw band that frustrated many citizens because they seemed immune from capture. Jeff Milton was an ex–Texas Ranger with a well-deserved reputation for integrity and proficiency with a gun. He was employed as a guard for the railroad and would ride the routes and protect the strong box. The other players in the drama that cold winter evening were Three Fingered Jack Dunlop, a cruel, vicious outlaw; Bravo Juan Yaos, another outlaw wanted on both sides of the border; and two brothers whose names have been lost to history.

As an officer of the law, Bill Stiles discovered Jeff Milton would not be guarding the strong box on the targeted train. What he could not know was that at the last minute, a sick employee prompted the company to substitute Milton on the run north from Mexico.

When the train arrived in Fairbank, the outlaw band posed as drunken cowboys and mingled with the crowd. Milton stood in the open door of the baggage car as freight was loaded and unloaded. The outlaws recognized Milton and opened fire. The former Texas lawman was struck twice in the arm. Unable to return fire for fear of hitting innocent bystanders, Milton stumbled back in to the baggage car and retrieved a shotgun with his good arm.

The bandits charged the train car after they saw Milton fall. The return fire from Milton was deadly; Three Fingered Jack was struck in the chest and Yaos was shot in the back as the outlaws turned to flee.

As the outlaws riddled the car with gunfire, Milton tossed the keys for the strong box into the night and made a tourniquet from his shirt. The frustrated outlaws had no choice but to flee with the armed men from Fairbank on their heels.

Three Fingered Jack was abandoned by his comrades and discovered in the brush nine miles from Fairbank. He lived long enough to make a confession and name his accomplices, who later received lengthy prison terms. Milton recovered, although he never regained full use of his arm. He was hired by the U.S. Immigration Service and patrolled the border. Milton died in 1947 at the age of eighty-five.

Fairbank slipped into obscurity with the closure of the railroad and mines in Tombstone and the milling at Contention City. An Arizona guide from 1940 noted a population of fifty. The school closed in 1944, and the post office that originally opened in 1883 closed in 1973.

In 1987, the town received a last minute reprieve from total abandonment when the Bureau of Land Management incorporated it into the San Pedro Riparian National Conservation Area. Efforts to retain what remained of the adobe commercial building that housed the post office were successful. The schoolhouse that was built in 1920 to replace the original destroyed by fire is now a visitor center and museum.

Jeff Davis Milton fell through the cracks in the annals of the western frontier's history. Considering his amazing and lengthy career, this obscurity is truly amazing.

In 1876, at the age of fifteen, Milton moved from Florida and went west to work in a mercantile store owned by a distant relative. This venture was short-lived. The lust for adventure led him to try his hand as a cowboy, where he proved himself adept as a horseman and proficient with guns.

His career in law enforcement began with the Texas Rangers. He lied about his age when he signed up because he was three years shy of the minimum requirement.

Milton patrolled the wild and wooly Big Bend country for three years. On more than one occasion, his gun skills literally were the difference between life and death.

When he left the Rangers, he attempted to settle into a quiet life. Yet after a brief stint homesteading a small ranch in New Mexico, he returned to law enforcement as a deputy sheriff and sheriff in numerous counties throughout the New Mexico and Arizona territories.

Milton's adventurous career also included a position as the collector of customs in the Nogales, Arizona, area; chief of police in El Paso, Texas; and Wells Fargo railroad agent. After he recovered from the injuries sustained in Fairbank, under direct commission from President Theodore Roosevelt, he patrolled the Arizona border as the Mounted Chinese Inspector for the Immigration Service. In 1919, Milton's work for the Immigration Service culminated with an unusual assignment: guard for a large number of arrested radicals and anarchists who were being deported to Russia.

## WHEN YOU GO

*From Tombstone, drive north for 3 miles on State Highway 80. Turn west on State Highway 82 and drive 7 miles.*

# G H O S T S  O F
# CENTRAL
# ARIZONA

OBSCURE BUT PIVOTAL MOMENTS IN HISTORY make Graham County unique. On the reservation at San Carlos, Geronimo initiated his war to reclaim the Apache homeland. Duncan figures prominently in the story of Black Jack Ketchum and Sandra Day O'Connor, the retired Supreme Court Justice.

In Maricopa County, the present and future are framed by the past with Wickenburg at the north end, Gila Bend to the south, and Phoenix and Buckeye in between. Here, centuries are mere moments in time since there have been farming communities along the Salt River for more than a thousand years.

The back roads of Yavapai County are a wonderland littered with partial ghosts, complete ghosts, and even intact stage roads. Here, too, is the territorial capital of Arizona and engineering marvels.

Most of this county consists of high mountains and forested valleys, making late spring, summer, and fall the best times to explore most of the ghosts here. There is no better time than the months of winter for seeking the wonders of Maricopa County and the desert valleys.

Farming was the cornerstone for life in Bonita, as evidenced by abandoned equipment, broken windmills, and weathered barns.

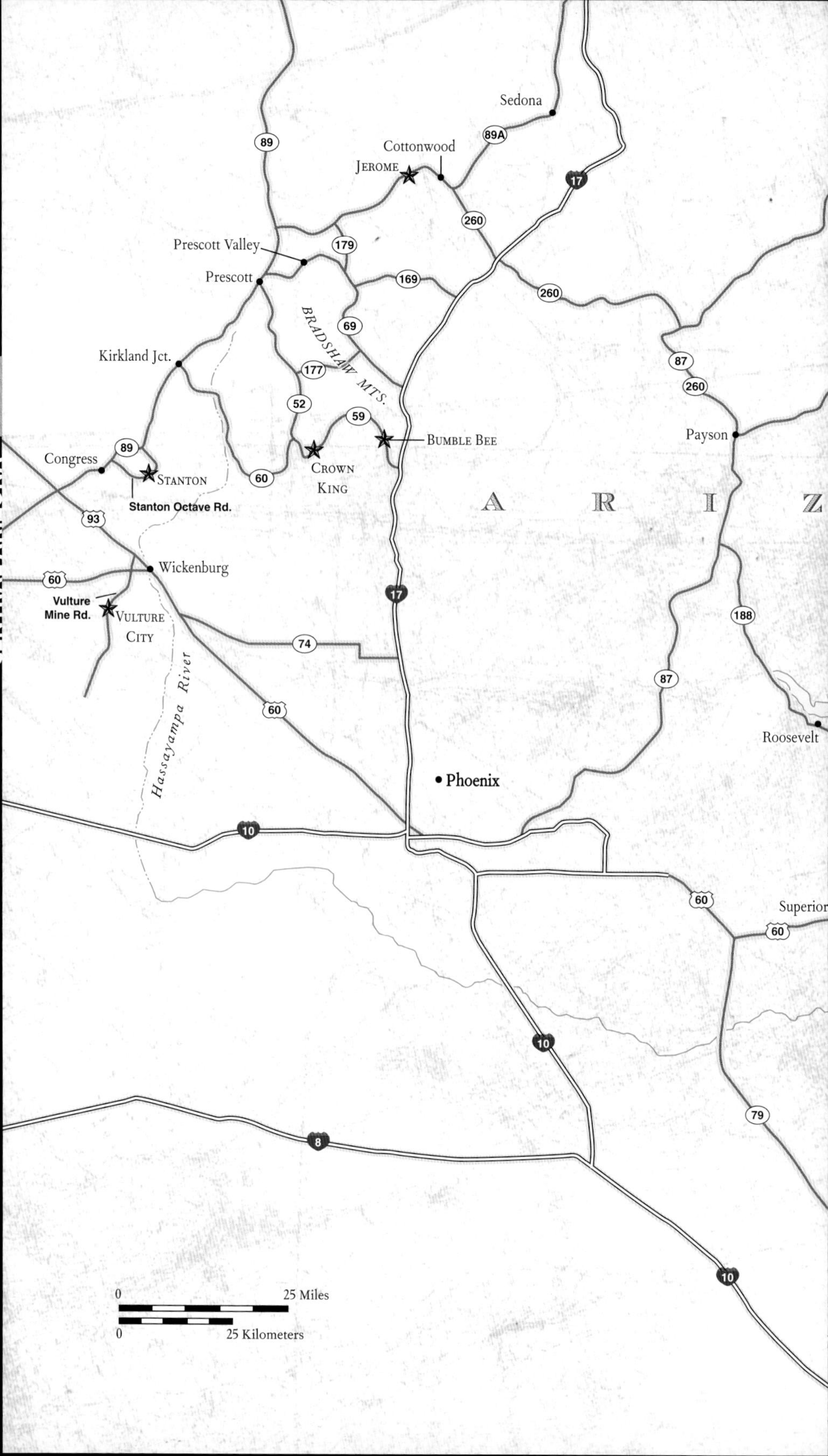

89

Sedona

89A

Cottonwood

JEROME

17

260

Prescott Valley

179

Prescott

169

BRADSHAW MTS.

69

260

Kirkland Jct.

177

87

260

52

Payson

59

89

Congress

BUMBLE BEE

STANTON

CROWN
KING

A       R       I       Z

Stanton Octave Rd.

93

60

Wickenburg

Vulture
Mine Rd.

VULTURE
CITY

74

188

60

87

Hassayampa River

Roosevelt

60

Phoenix

10

60

Superior

60

10

8

79

10

0                    25 Miles

0                    25 Kilometers

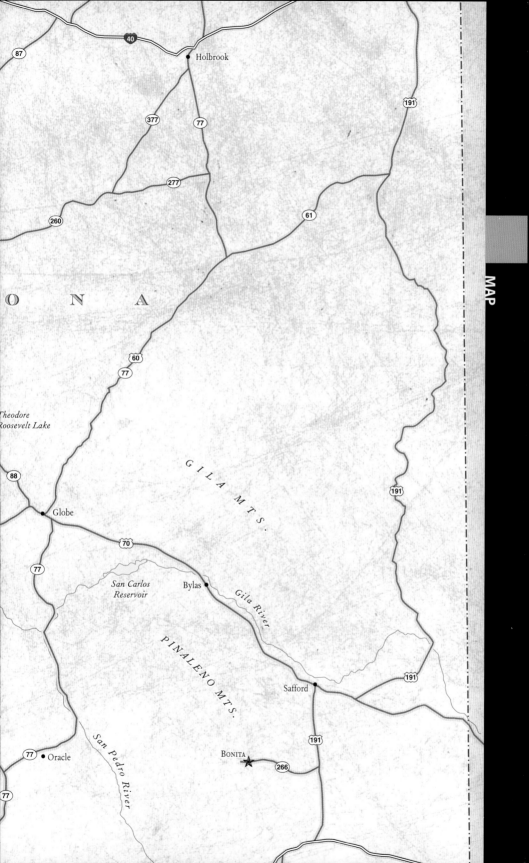

# BONITA

Ruins and the beauty of the Aravaipa Valley with the Pinaleno Mountains as a backdrop are primary features in Bonita today. There is, however, one remaining building of particular note: the two-story general store.

In 1877, the building was George Atkins' saloon. In August of that year, Francis P. Cahill, a strapping Irish laborer and itinerant blacksmith, made the fatal mistake of bullying scrawny Henry Antrim in the street in front of the saloon. The taunting ended in a roar and flash of smoke with Cahill lying mortally wounded in the street.

Antrim was just another rootless kid and an unknown among the thousands of young men wandering the West in search of adventure or a better life. Yet this anonymity would be short-lived, as Antrim would become better known as William H. Bonney and later as Billy the Kid.

Ranching and military forces were the lifeblood of Bonita. Cowboys from nearby ranches, such as the sprawling Sierra Bonita that was owned by Henry Hooker, and soldiers from Fort Grant a few miles to the north made the town a lively place.

The Bonita store represents one of the last artifacts from a once vital and bustling business district, which included numerous stores, restaurants, and a boarding house.

Bonita and nearby Fort Grant were prominently featured in two historic events. In March 1871, several hundred Apaches (the majority being elderly men, women, and children) were at a camp between Bonita and Fort Grant under the care of Lieutenant Royal Whitman, the camp's commander. These refugees received exceptional care in the hope it would encourage the warring Apaches to surrender.

Erroneous information led Tucson citizens to believe the Native Americans at Fort Grant were the members of the band responsible for the devastating raids through the Santa Cruz Valley. On April 28, 1871, more than one hundred riders, including civic leaders from Tucson, Papago Indians, and Mexicans, rode out from Tucson. They raided the Apache camp several days later and killed most of its inhabitants.

The commanders at Fort Grant buried the dead and began a public relations campaign to convince the Apaches that the raid was not the work of the U.S. Army. The tragedy sparked outrage throughout the country, and President Ulysses S. Grant ordered the territorial governor to find those who were responsible for the raid. The leaders were brought to trial and acquitted in spite of the outcry.

The second historic event near Bonita and Fort Grant occurred on May 11, 1889. An ambush on the road between Fort Grant and Fort Thomas relieved Major Joseph Wham, an army paymaster, and his Tenth Calvary escort of $26,000. Seven of the eleven-man escort group were wounded. Sergeant Ben Brown and Corporal Isaiah Mays, African-American soldiers assigned to this unit, were able to travel to a nearby ranch to get help, even though they were under heavy fire. Both men received the Medal of Honor for their bravery and sacrifice.

Today Bonita is a quiet dusty wide spot in the road. Fort Grant exists only as a name on the map and is now a part of the Arizona state prison system.

## WHEN YOU GO

*From Safford, drive 17 miles south on U.S. Highway 191. Turn west on Arizona Highway 266, and drive for 17 miles.*

# VULTURE CITY

By the early 1860s, a number of American prospecting parties had followed the Hassayampa River into the Bradshaw Mountains to find the next big mining vein and had various degrees of success. However, none of these discoveries came close to the one made by Henry Wickenburg in 1863.

Rather than incur the astronomical cost of shipping and milling raw ore, Wickenburg wisely chose to sell it from his Vulture Mine for fifteen dollars per ton and let the buyer worry about those formalities. Because water was a scarce commodity at the Vulture Mine, a town named for the Austrian-born discoverer of the mine mushroomed along the banks of the Hassayampa River about eleven miles to the north. Wickenburg had a supportive infrastructure, including a mill, to alleviate the water problem at the mine.

After the Central Arizona Mining Company acquired controlling interest in the property, a six-inch pipeline that ran for twelve miles from the Hassayampa to the Vulture Mine was constructed. A state-of-the-art eighty stamp mill was also constructed on site to eliminate the expense of hauling raw ore.

Before the new mill was built, the tailings of waste and low-grade ores were deemed too cost prohibitive to process. After the mill was completed, the tailings became an asset. The original assay office was built from local stone and waste from the mine, but it, along with most of the other original buildings at the site, were later processed for their gold content.

In the fall of 1880, the small camp of hardworking miners and their families who were living in the shadow of the mine's head frame and mill received official recognition as Vulture City with the opening of a post office. The population had risen to almost five hundred by 1889, and the Vulture Mine was the largest gold producer in the territory.

Vulture City's downward turn began in 1891. The vein in the main shaft abruptly ended at a fault. Failure to relocate the vein prompted the mine's sale, but the new owners had better luck. Shortly after the vein was reconnected, another fault resulted in costly exploratory work. This process continued for a short period until the frustrated and broke owners sold the mine. The new owners fared even worse. They literally brought the roof down when they tried to expand operations.

Many original buildings in Vulture City were recycled after the discovery that the stones with which they were constructed were valuable ore.

An effort to present Vulture City, a privately owned ghost town, in a state of preservation presents an eerie impression.

In Vulture City, as in most ghost towns, the desert slowly reclaims the evidence of past glory and covers those scars with cacti.

The post office closed in April 1897 and served as the post mortem for the once prosperous enterprise. There were numerous attempts to reopen the mine over the years that included sinking a new shaft in 1931 and aborted efforts to rework the tailings in late 1941.

Vulture City has survived into the modern era relatively intact as the result of private ownership. Sadly, the man who discovered the mine did not fare as well.

In 1865, Henry Wickenburg sold four-fifths interest in the mine for eighty-five thousand dollars. Wickenburg received twenty-five thousand dollars before a question pertaining to his title to the property led to lawsuits and a lengthy court battle. When the dust cleared, the initial twenty-five thousand dollars was all Wickenburg received, and he spent most of the money on attorneys in a vain effort to recover the rest.

The hapless prospector spent the next forty years in a similar pattern. In 1905, after a flood devastated his small farm near Wickenburg, he committed suicide in the shade of a mesquite tree on the banks of the Hassayampa River.

## WHEN YOU GO

*Drive 2.5 miles west of Wickenburg on U.S. Highway 60. Turn south on Vulture Mine Road, and continue for 12 miles. The current owners allow self-guided tours, but there are no set hours and there is an admission charge to visit the property.*

Legend is that the "jail tree" did double duty, with outlaws chained to its stout trunk and as a lynching post for miscreants in Wickenburg and Vulture City.

# STANTON

Pauline Weaver was a renowned trapper and guide in the Arizona Territory during the early 1860s. When he announced he would be leading a party up the Hassayampa River into the Bradshaw Mountains in 1862, a long list of men wanted to accompany Weaver on his trek. At the top of a granite knoll, a landmark later listed as Rich Hill, Weaver and his party discovered the richest placer discovery

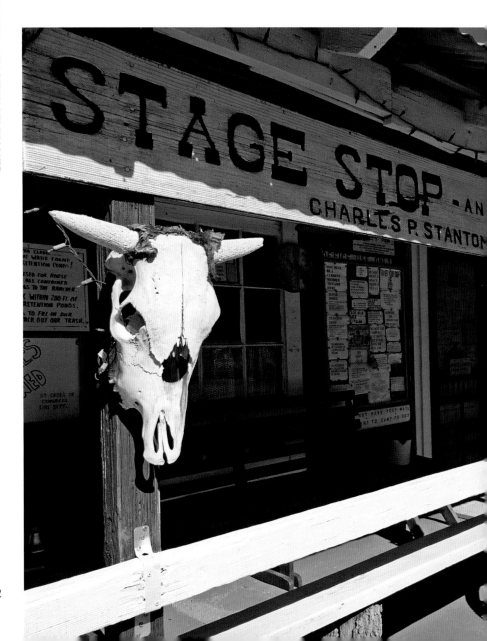

in Arizona history. According to legend, the Weaver party, with little more than knives and the toes of their boots, had gathered almost one hundred thousand

The old mining camp has been given a new lease on life as an RV park bearing modern amenities for the prospectors of the twenty-first century.

A surprising number of vestiges from Stanton's past have survived into the modern era, presenting the illusion that this town is a forlorn time capsule.

dollars in loose nuggets and flakes within a few weeks. This discovery sparked a gold rush into the Arizona Territory.

Several years after the discovery, Charles Stanton established a store and station on the stage line that ran through the valley in the shadow of Rich Hill.

The two businesses, in conjunction with a half interest in the nearby Leviathan Mine (an investment acquired through questionable means while he was working in the assay office at the Vulture Mine), provided a comfortable living. Stanton, however, suffered from an extreme case of greed.

With the right amount of photographic slight of hand, the buildings in Stanton appear as a portal into an earlier time.

Weathered boots on a weathered wall in Stanton reflect the tough qualities of the pioneers who first wrestled gold from the surrounding mountains.

As the collection of tents and shacks gave way to houses and stores, the area became a real community known as Antelope Station. As the community grew, Stanton's holdings increased proportionally to the number of competitors who disappeared or who sold their properties to Stanton for a bargain price. Many people in the area suspected that his ostentatious lifestyle was funded with more than his many business interests provided.

By 1875, the camp dwarfed its neighbors, Octave and Weaver, and Stanton had the town renamed after him with the approval of a post office application. The town of Stanton was at its peak fifteen years later with several hundred residents, a five stamp mill, and a thriving business district. However, one resident who was conspicuously absent from town in 1890 was Charles Stanton.

Frontier justice was often swift in Arizona's territorial years, and few bad men lived long enough to enjoy their ill-gotten gains. On November 13, 1886, Pedro Lucero, a member of a gang used by Stanton for nefarious activities, corrected an insult to his sister in Stanton's store with two well-placed shots.

Today, visitors to Stanton, Octave, and Weaver will find little more than ruins, mine tailings, and scenery. A prospectors club has transformed much of the mining camp into an RV park for those who seek desert solitude or wish to try their hand at prospecting. Many of the surviving structures are being refurbished to provide services for campers, including a library and game room.

## WHEN YOU GO

*From Wickenburg, drive 6 miles north on U.S. Highway 93 and turn north on U.S. Highway 89. Three miles north of Congress, turn left onto the Stanton Octave Road and continue approximately 7 miles. Road conditions depend on the time between the most recent rain and grading. The best time for visiting or exploring is in late fall, early spring, or winter.*

# BUMBLE BEE

The origins of the town's unusual name are lost to history, as well as the date its location was first settled and the exact name of the founder. What is known is the dependable creek and lush pasture at the location led a detachment of U.S. Cavalry to establish a temporary outpost at the site of present-day Bumble Bee. Later, W. (or W. W.) Snyder established a hostelry and stable to meet the needs of travelers, utilizing a new stage line between Prescott and Phoenix.

The stop was labeled Snyder's Station and became a key supply center for the area with the explosion of mineral discoveries and development of mines in the nearby Bradshaw Mountains.

The discovery of placer deposits scattered among the gravel beds in nearby streams and dry arroyos fueled the area's growth. By late 1878, the station had morphed into a small settlement, and in February of the following year, approval for a post office application transformed Snyder's Station into Bumble Bee.

Bumble Bee is not a true ghost, as a few individuals still dwell among the ruins and shells surrounded by stunning natural beauty.

In Bumble Bee, the past, present, and future seem to meld together as remnants from the distant past blend with re-creations of the modern era.

Against a backdrop of cloud towers that hint of a coming storm, the last remnants of Bumble Bee appear timeless.

The fortunes of Bumble Bee rose and fell with the prosperity of the area mines and nearby mining camps. In 1895, the completion of a rail line that connected Phoenix with the main line at Ashfork via Prescott effectively ended the stage and freight service that was the lifeblood of the little community.

Bumble Bee received a new lease on life with motorists making the drive from Phoenix to Prescott until the 1940s. With the construction of the Black Canyon Highway, State Highway 769, and the Interstate 17 bypass of the steep grades of Antelope Hill, Bumble Bee became a ghost town.

In 1949, and again in 1960, the town site was sold to new owners who planned to resurrect the town as a tourist attraction. Some old buildings received false fronts, new buildings mimicked the same theme, and others collapsed into photogenic ruin.

Today Bumble Bee is off-limits to exploration without permission from the owners, and several old buildings are occupied residences. Large sections of the town still front State Highway 59.

## WHEN YOU GO

*From Phoenix, drive 55 miles north on Interstate 17 to exit number 248. Follow Bumble Bee Road/State Highway 59 toward Crown King and drive approximately 8 miles.*

# CROWN KING

Crown King is the sole survivor among the many mining camps that sprang up in the rugged, sprawling Bradshaw Mountains. It is also is home to one of the great engineering marvels of the Old West.

Bill and Ike Bradshaw operated a successful freighting business that traveled from San Bernardino, California, to mining camps in the Mojave Desert and also included a ferry service to the river ports of Ehrenberg and La Paz. In the late 1860s, the operations were expanded to include service to Prescott.

Bill discovered ore on the road to Prescott and sparked a boom that became one of the largest in the territory to that date. By 1871, the entire Bradshaw mining district had exploded with activity, as mines and supportive camps sprang up throughout the mountains.

Millions of dollars in gold and silver flowed from the Tip Top, Columbia, Oro Belle, Big Bug, Crown King, Senator, and Bueno mines. Towns like Bradshaw City soon boasted of populations that numbered in the thousands.

The bat wing doors framing the entrance to the saloon in Crown King enhance the time-capsule feel of this rare tangible link to the frontier era.

The boom was relatively short-lived, and by the early 1880s, most of the towns were less than ghosts because the buildings had been dismantled and rebuilt in other camps. By the late 1890s, only Crown King remained as a viable community.

Frank Murphy was a pioneering railroad tycoon with a long record of transforming the impossible into the possible and profitable. He was also a man who possessed the uncanny ability to spot an opportunity. The manifestation of these talents came with his decision to connect the profitable mines at Crown King with the main railroad line that ran from Prescott to Phoenix.

The promise of one dollar a day, which was twice the standard wage, lured experienced tracklayers from throughout the country, as well as Europe and Australia. In October 1901, work commenced on a project that was deemed impossible because of its difficult engineering.

When a dynamite blast exposed a rich deposit of placer gold in April 1902, many men quit and were consumed with gold fever. In spite of these obstacles, the branch line of the Prescott & Eastern Railroad to Crown King opened for business in 1904.

The railroad line was an amazing accomplishment. The line traversed numerous arroyos from Mayer to Cordes and traveled across Crazy Basin. A series of switchbacks were so sharp they required modified rolling stock for the

*Above and opposite:* Crown King is alive and well, thanks in part to the busy saloon, which was relocated from Bradshaw City more than a century ago.

last thirteen miles. There was a three thousand–foot rise in elevation between the destinations.

The rails are now gone, but the rail bed—with its curves, narrow bridges, and awe-inspiring views—is the primary road to Crown King. A secondary road is the old Senator Highway from Prescott, which is an unforgettable journey of less than forty miles but requires at least three hours to travel in good weather and a solid vehicle with good ground clearance.

The Senator Highway is a rare opportunity to experience a real frontier highway as it was back in the day. The rocky old road climbs through the forest that hugs the steep hillsides, fords several small streams, and even passes an authentic log-constructed stage station that dates to the 1870s.

Frank Murphy made many contributions to the development of the Arizona Territory. One engineering marvel of his was the railroad to Crown King.

In 1892, Murphy initiated construction of a railroad to link the main line at Ashfork with Prescott. From this Peavine line, a branch built into Clarkdale initiated the expansion of mining in Jerome.

The next endeavor was a line that linked Prescott with Phoenix. The completion of this 136-mile line in March 1895 was considered the official closing of the frontier period in Arizona.

The scenic Crown King cemetery presents the illusion that this ghost, among the towering pines of the Bradshaw Mountains, is another forgotten mining camp.

## WHEN YOU GO

There are two routes to Crown King: the Senator Highway and the old rail bed. The latter is the primary route and is the only one accessible by passenger cars, although it is a gravel road. From Phoenix, drive north on Interstate 17 to exit 248 (Bumble Bee) and follow the signs for 28 miles.

The ink of the World War I armistice was barely dry when the mines began to close at Crown King. Production no longer warranted a railroad to the remote mountain community, and in 1926 the rail bed became an automobile road. The last of the company-owned mines closed in 1942.

Crown King hung on by a thread with a few residents working small claims and others who offered limited service to the residents from the desert below who came to escape the heat. That trend continues today.

The saloon relocated from Bradshaw City is still in operation, as is the post office/general store that serves as the sole service station. The rest of the town is a smattering of original buildings, a few new summer homes, and a new restaurant built from the remains of the old stamp mill.

Nestled among the towering pines along the Senator Highway is the Palace Station, a truly rare gem that is one of the few remaining authentic stagecoach stations in the state of Arizona. This delightful time capsule is more than a tangible link to the frontier era of the Arizona Territory—it is also a portal into an earlier time.

In 1875, Alfred Spence; his wife, Matilde; and his father-in-law relocated from nearby Groom Creek to Crooks Canyon and constructed a primary log structure. The board-and-batten kitchen was added in 1890. Nothing has changed to the building, with the exception of the rear porch.

When the Spences first built their house, only a mule trail connected Crooks Canyon to the Senator Road between Prescott and the Senator Mine. In 1877, a wagon road from Prescott to Phoenix through the Bradshaw mining district transformed the Spence homestead into the Palace Station.

Traffic along the road was brisk. Stagecoaches, freighters, mule skinners, and prospectors on foot all found an oasis at the Palace Station. The last travelers to use the station's services arrived by automobile.

The station reverted to its role as a family homestead in 1910. In 1963, the Prescott National Forest assumed custodial control of this historical treasure.

# JEROME

Nevada had the Comstock Lode, Colorado had Cripple Creek, and Arizona had Jerome. Before the mines permanently closed in 1953, Jerome perched precariously on the slopes of Cleopatra Hill and featured million-dollar views of the Verde Valley, which became known as the "billion-dollar copper camp."

The amazing story of this ghost city begins in 1583 with the explorations of Antonio de Espejo, the discovery of silver in the hills above the valley, and evidence of previous mining. Explorations followed in 1598 and 1604, but the remote location and rugged terrain prevented development of the finds for more than two centuries.

In the early 1870s, Al Sieber, a scout for the U.S. Army, began working claims on Cleopatra Hill in an area that bore evidence of the older exploratory work. By 1882, mining on the cone-shaped treasure trove that was Cleopatra Hill was in full swing, and a roughshod mining camp was quickly spreading along the flanks of the hill.

Jerome, spread along the slopes of Cleopatra Hill in the Mingus Mountains, is Arizona's "ghost city" with a population in the hundreds.

Buildings constructed of cut stone and brick give clear indication that Jerome was once a city with great promise.

John and Ed O'Dougherty and John Boyd, with financial backing by Territorial Governor Fred Tritle and Bill Murray, all worked the claim. The partners needed money to further develop the property and turned to Eugene Jerome, a wealthy New York financier whose cousin was Jennie Jerome, mother to Winston Churchill.

The new venture, the United Verde Mine, extracted an amazing eighty thousand dollars in silver in 1883, also the year the mining camp officially became known as Jerome thanks to the establishment of a post office. The cost of transporting ore to the rail line at Ashfork was twenty dollars per ton and prohibitive to all but the richest deposits. This fact, along with the exhaustion of the primary ore body in 1884, led to an almost complete abandonment of the fledgling mining camp.

In 1888, William Clark, a Montana mining magnate, purchased the United Verde Mine and several other properties. In 1892, Clark financed the construction of a narrow gauge rail line from Jerome Junction, now Chino Valley, to Jerome, and the boom was on.

Fires swept through Jerome in 1897, 1898, and 1899, but after every fire, the community was rebuilt on a larger and grander scale with hotels such as the Montana, a plush two hundred–room palace that offered amenities equal to any hotel in New York or San Francisco; a state-of-the-art hospital; blocks of offices and stores; and mansions. In 1920, a highway carved from the slopes of Mingus Mountain linked Prescott and Jerome to further fuel the town's growth and led to the development of businesses that provided "modern" services to travelers.

When the stock market crashed in 1929, the population had reached its pinnacle of fifteen thousand. The collapse of copper prices led to the closure of the United Verde Mine. It reopened in 1935, but the town's downturn had begun.

The mines closed again in 1950, and abandonment of the city began in earnest. By the mid-1960s, the population had dwindled to a few hundred souls residing among the ruins that framed spectacular views. However, the ghost city of Jerome began to experience a rebirth of sorts as eclectic artists and tourists discovered these stunning vistas, picturesque ruins, and the delightful territorial-styled architecture of the remaining buildings.

Like most frontier-era mining camps, Jerome had its share of colorful characters, but what makes this one of the most fascinating ghost towns in the Southwest today is the unique character of the town. First, Jerome offers panoramic views of the Verde River Valley and the red rock country of Sedona to the north. Also large

The rising sun's golden glow gives the towering Jerome ruins a sense of timelessness.

Years of underground blasting shook many buildings in Jerome, including the jail, from their foundations, which resulted in their slide down the steep mountain slopes.

The rendering of iron into artistic fencing painted with the patina of age adds a classical feeling to Jerome's ruins and cemetery.

Jerome was and is a marvel of ingenious, gravity-defying construction that led to the unofficial slogan of "America's Most Unique City." *Author collection*

portions of the town have become a slide zone for remaining buildings, the result of extensive underground blasting in the 1920s that loosened buildings from their foundations. As an example, the jail has slid more than two hundred feet down the steep slope of Cleopatra Hill.

Adding to the allure is Jerome's wide array of attractions. The beautiful Douglas Mansion is the centerpiece of the Jerome State Historic Park. The home of the chief surgeon for the Little Daisy Mine is a delightful bed and breakfast. Dining options run the gamut from simple fare in original cafés—including the English Kitchen that dates to 1899 and is the oldest continuously operated restaurant in Arizona—to five-star meals in a former speakeasy.

## WHEN YOU GO

*From Prescott, go north on 89 for 5 miles and take a right onto Highway 89A. Follow 89A for 29 miles to Jerome.*

133

# GHOSTS OF
# NORTHERN ARIZONA

CREATED IN 1891, COCONINO COUNTY ENCOMPASSES some of Arizona's most famous landmarks, including the Grand Canyon. Ranching, logging, the railroad, and eventually Route 66 dominated the era of frontier and prewar development in this area.

Vast ranching empires left a colorful legacy but few discernable links, with the exception of the ranches themselves, many of which are still in operation. Railroad camps were often temporary in nature and left little to mark their passing. The lumber mills were very much the same.

One of the most fascinating survivors has a storied history that connects the era of the boundless frontier with that of Route 66. Another survivor is a mysterious connection to a lost civilization sheltered by awe-inspiring walls of colorful stone.

A modern addition to the ruins of Two Guns links them with iconic Route 66, the Main Street of America.

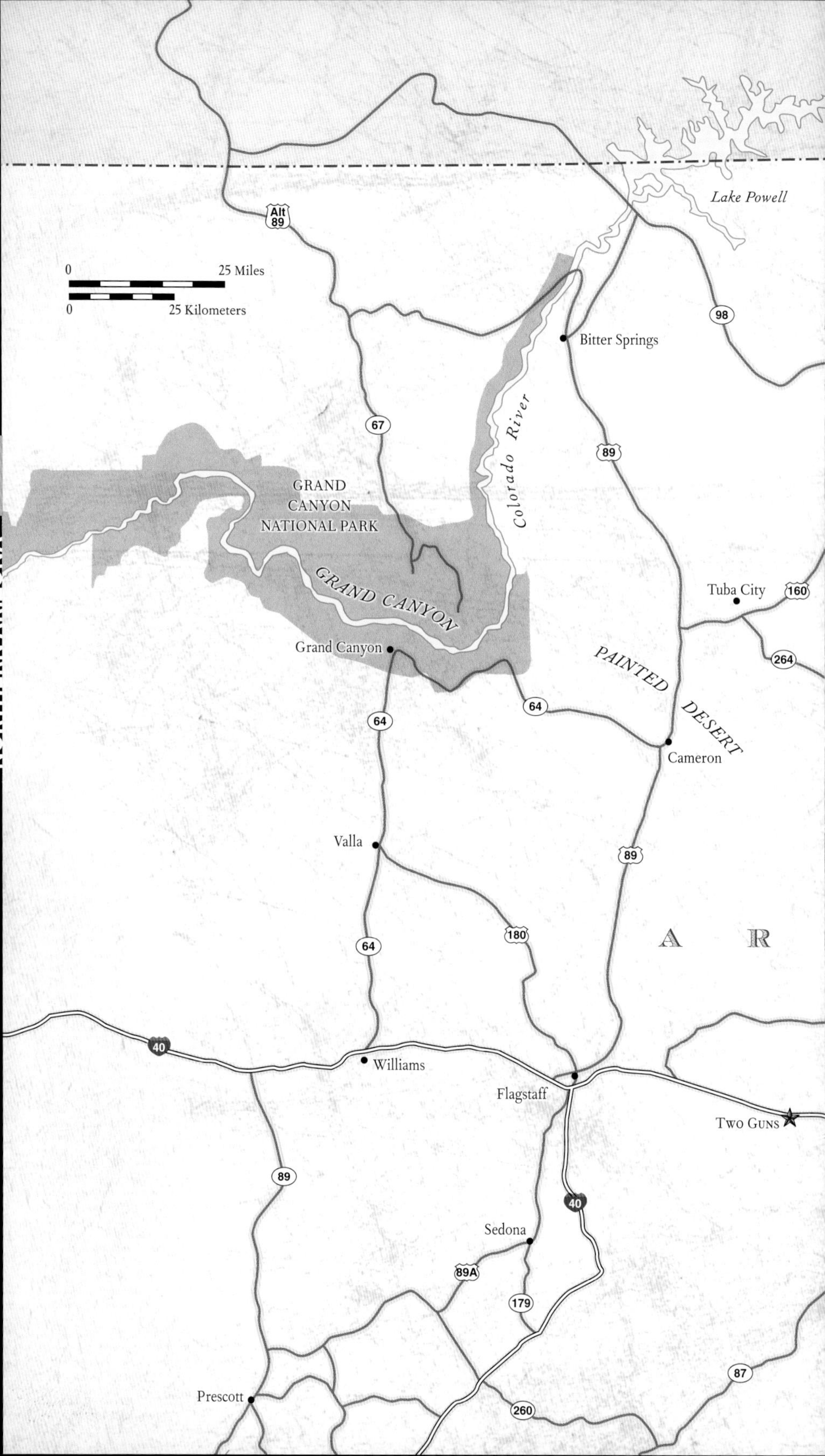

Alt
89

0                    25 Miles
0                    25 Kilometers

98

Bitter Springs

67

89

GRAND
CANYON
NATIONAL PARK

*Colorado River*

GRAND CANYON

Tuba City          160

Grand Canyon

*PAINTED*

264

64          64

*DESERT*

Cameron

Valla

89

64          180

A          R

40

Williams

Flagstaff

Two Guns

40

89

Sedona

89A

179

87

Prescott

260

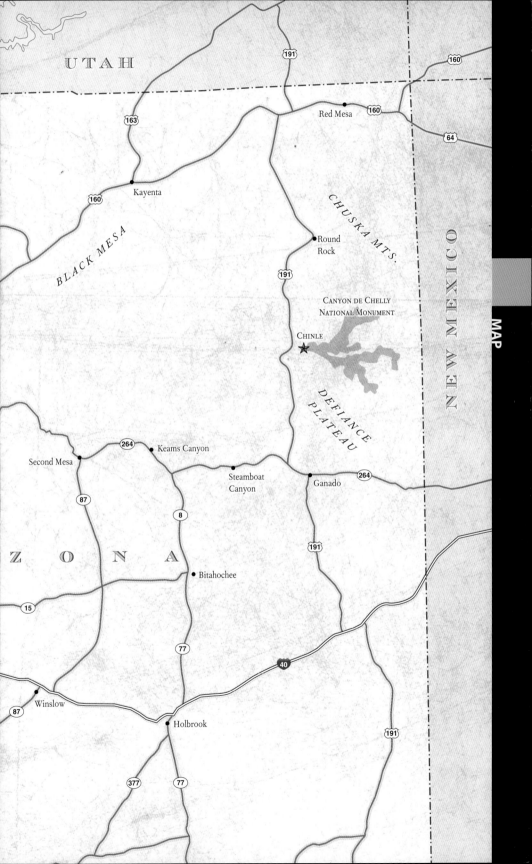

UTAH

NEW MEXICO

BLACK MESA

CHUSKA MTS.

DEFIANCE PLATEAU

Z   O   N   A

191

160

160

64

163

160   Kayenta

Red Mesa   160

Round Rock

191

CANYON DE CHELLY
NATIONAL MONUMENT

CHINLE

264   Keams Canyon

Second Mesa

Steamboat Canyon

Ganado   264

87

8

191

Bitahochee

15

77

40

191

87   Winslow

Holbrook

377   77

# TWO GUNS

In 1853, Lieutenant Amiel W. Whipple led a survey expedition along the thirty-fifth parallel through New Mexico and Arizona in an effort to determine the feasibility of constructing a southern transcontinental railroad. On December 14 of that year, Whipple noted, "We were all surprised to find at our feet, in magnesium limestone, a chasm probably one hundred feet in depth [author's note: it was actually 250 feet], the sides precipitous, and about three hundred feet across." He also noted, "For a railroad it could be bridged and the banks would furnish plenty of stone for the purpose." This was Canyon Diablo.

Despite delays initiated by the Civil War, construction of the proposed railroad reached this daunting chasm in 1880. Engineers thought it would be more efficient to build the timber portions of the bridge in sections at another location because lumber was scarce on the high desert plains. Once the bridge was assembled, it was short by several feet and added comic relief to the challenging project.

The skeletons of gas pumps in Two Guns commemorate the era of tail fins, Edsels, and the golden age of the road trip.

As construction commenced, a small settlement consisting largely of canvas-roofed adobe saloons, shacks, and rough abodes carved from the pockets in the walls of the canyon developed on the eastern side of the bridge. The town of Canyon Diablo was a recreation center for gandy dancers, cowboys, and railroad crews and was not a quiet place.

The lawlessness of Canyon Diablo was exemplified in the fact there were several train robberies in the immediate area within a matter of months. One robbery contributed greatly to the fast-growing legend of Bucky O'Neill, a former soldier and newspaper editor turned sheriff. He and a three-man posse pursued the robbers through six hundred miles of the roughest country in the Southwest before they were captured at the Utah border.

By 1900, the camp was little more than a pile of melting adobe ruins, a wide debris field, and the trading post of Fred Volz. Surprisingly, a few residents still called the canyon pockets home. One of these men, "Two Gun" Miller, became a prominent figure in the next chapter of the area's history.

Miller claimed to be many things over the years, including an Apache, but all who encountered him agreed that he was crazy and violent. A number of factors, including the murder of a neighbor that was ruled as self-defense, fostered this opinion.

With the rise of tourism and the completion of a bridge for the National Old Trails Highway, later known as Route 66, in 1926, an enterprising entrepreneur capitalized on the legend of "Two Gun" Miller by establishing the Canyon Lodge on the edge of the canyon about a mile south of the railroad crossing. Two Guns eventually became a tourist oasis with a small zoo, Apache caves, a gas station, a store, and other facilities.

Access to the extensive ruins of Two Guns, with its 1914-era concrete bridge spanning the chasm, and to the site of Canyon Diablo is subject to the whim of the current owner. However, most of the ruins at Two Guns are visible from Interstate 40.

## WHEN YOU GO

*From Winslow, take Interstate 40 west and travel for 21 miles to exit 230.*

William O. "Buckey" O'Neill was a product of the western frontier. He was intelligent, colorful, flamboyant, and fearless. These attributes served him well as a newspaperman, politician, and sheriff of Yavapai County.

When Teddy Roosevelt began recruiting his Rough Riders during the Spanish-American War, the irrepressible O'Neill was among the first to sign up. The fearless tenacity that made him a favorite son of the Arizona Territory led him to the front lines of most major battles in Cuba as the captain of Company A.

O'Neill's motto was, "An officer should always set an example to his men." It was also his epitaph.

Despite exposure to enemy fire that felled several officers in the battle of Las Guasimas, he left the field unscathed. In smaller skirmishes, his bravado and luck again delivered him from harm. A sniper's bullet in the battle of San Juan Hill ended his audacious career and lucky streak. An imposing statue of O'Neill on horseback dominates the courthouse square in Prescott.

The men who rode for the brand of the Hash Knife Cattle Company were a motley bunch. A man's ability to perform the grueling tasks of a cowboy went further toward landing the job than his character or virtue. As a result, more than a few of the hired hands were wanted fugitives with a lengthy list of aliases.

The rowdy and deadly exploits of these cowboys made Tombstone seem a refined place compared to Winslow and Holbrook. John Shaw's farewell party at Canyon Diablo speaks volumes about the nature of these men.

On April 9, 1905, Navajo County Sheriff Chet Houck and Deputy Pete Pemberton followed two men suspected of robbing the Wigwam Saloon in Winslow. The suspected robbers rode to Canyon Diablo, and a confrontation led to a classic western shootout. When the smoke cleared, one outlaw, John Shaw, was dead on the street and the other was a wounded prisoner.

Several days later, more than a dozen inebriated cowboys from the Hash Knife outfit who rode with Shaw took the train from Winslow to Canyon Diablo for a farewell party. After the cowboys secured a box camera and a shovel at gunpoint from Fred Volz's trading post, they dug up Shaw, who was buried without ceremony, leaned him against a fence, and poured a drink between his teeth. Afterwards they reburied him with the half-finished bottle of whiskey.

# CANYON DE CHELLY

Canyon de Chelly is not your typical ghost town. In fact, it is not actually a town in the traditional sense but rather a series of communal housing and ceremonial complexes in a gorgeous setting. It is also unique in that its relevance and importance have spanned more than a thousand years.

The walls at the entrance to Canyon de Chelly are about thirty feet in height, but they stretch for one thousand feet and higher within a few miles. The Anasazi utilized pockets in the canyon walls to construct structures that are amazing engineering marvels.

Antelope House is a massive ninety-room complex intricately woven to fit the rock face and overhang. The White House Ruin consists of sixty rooms in the lower section and twenty tucked into a cave in the cliff face. The intersecting Canyon del Muerto also contains extensive ruins.

The expansive ruins in Canyon de Chelly are dwarfed by the magnitude of the stone spires and canyon walls that embrace them.

The weathered rock walls that shelter the ruins in Canyon de Chelly appear as impregnable battlements.

The landscape of Canyon de Chelly overwhelms the senses with an unequaled majestic beauty.

The primary years of construction and occupation of these, as well as the other ruins in the canyon complex, were between A.D. 1060 and 1275. In the centuries that followed, the ruins and the valleys served a variety of purposes. Perhaps the most notable use of the ruins was as a fort in January 1864 during the final battle between Navajo warriors and U.S. Army troops under command of General James Henry Carleton. The Navajo carefully chose Canyon de Chelly and Canyon del Muerto as the location for their final stand because of its strategic and cultural significance.

The extensive ruins and stunning landscape consistently rank as one of the most scenic attractions in America by a wide array of travel writers. Maps are available at the visitor center in Chinle for the rim drives. The canyon complex can only be explored with a guide.

## WHEN YOU GO

*The Canyon de Chelly National Park is located on U.S. Highway 191 in the town of Chinle.*

# GHOSTS OF
# NORTHERN NEW MEXICO

THE GHOSTS OF NORTHERN NEW MEXICO ARE A DIVERSE LOT. They run the gamut from remnants of lost civilizations to once prosperous gold mining towns nestled against snow-covered peaks and Spanish colonial outposts in desert sands, with plethoras of quaint, centuries-old villages; pueblos that are even older; and colonial settlements that are now cities in between. Add some of the most beautiful and breathtaking scenery in the country, and hunting for these ghost towns easily becomes a series of unforgettable vacations. It is also an excellent introduction to discover why New Mexico is the land of enchantment.

The hollow stone ruins of the Mutz Hotel and dance hall offer the only hint that this site was once one of the most promising communities in the Territory of New Mexico.

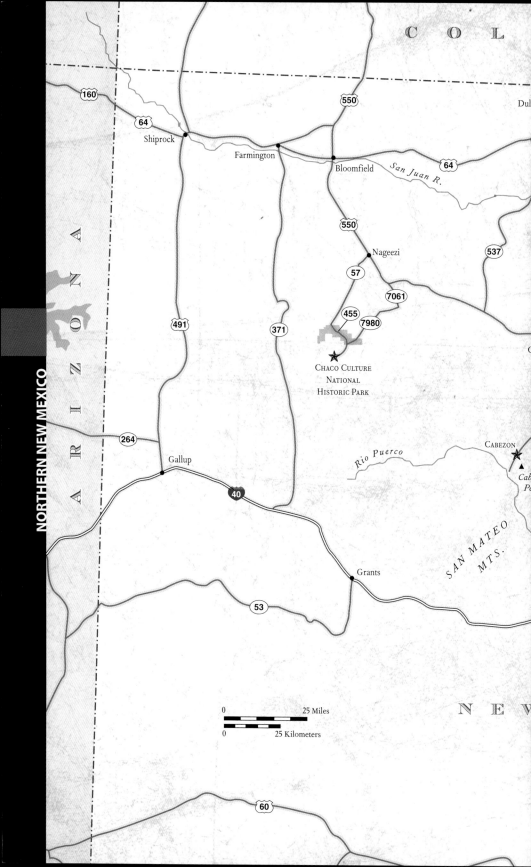

C O L

160

64

Shiprock

Farmington

Bloomfield

San Juan R.

550

64

Dul

550

Nageezi

537

57

7061

455

7980

CHACO CULTURE
NATIONAL
HISTORIC PARK

491

371

264

CABEZON

Gallup

Rio Puerco

Cab
Pa

40

SAN MATEO

MTS.

Grants

53

N E V

0        25 Miles

0        25 Kilometers

60

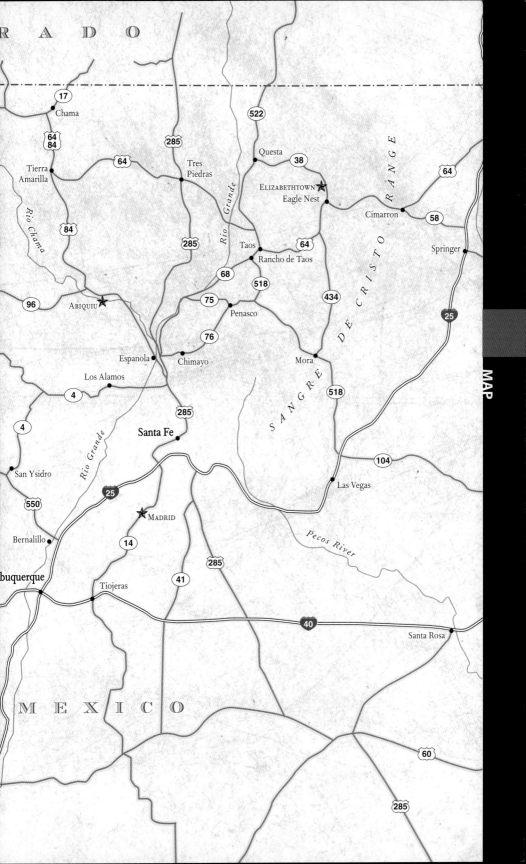

# CHACO CANYON

The breathtaking landscapes of northwestern New Mexico became more spectacular with each passing day to Lieutenant James Hervey Simpson and his survey party in the late summer of 1849. One morning in August, the guides led them to the most wondrous site they had yet encountered: imposing stone towers that were three stories in height in some places. This site was Pueblo Pintado, the portal to the treasures of Chaco Canyon.

Simpson marveled at the walls, engineering, and exquisite workmanship. He noted, "beautifully diminutive and true are all the details of the structure as to cause it, at a little distance, to have all of the appearance of a magnificent piece of mosaic work."

Eleven miles to the west, deep in Chaco Canyon surrounded by colorful canyon walls three hundred feet high, they discovered a vast complex of stone villages, each with high walls and a plaza. Pueblo Bonito was one village that had walls five stories in height and encompassed hundreds of rooms.

A variety of dating techniques indicate the complex prospered and grew for more than one hundred years, from roughly A.D. 1000 to the mid-1100s, when an extensive and lengthy drought transformed the landscape and devastated the farm-based economy. Further indications hint that before the droughts occurred, the complex of linked communities was an important trading center for villages hundreds of miles away.

Since Simpson's expedition, extensive exploration and numerous archaeological expeditions in Chaco Canyon have exposed a multitude of secrets. There have been more than thirty-five hundred archaeological sites identified in the canyon and surrounding area, more than four hundred miles of roads discovered that

## WHEN YOU GO

*From Albuquerque, drive 144 miles west on U.S. Highway 550. You will be able to follow the signs to the entrance for the last 21 miles. Food, camping gear, a full tank of gasoline, and a vehicle in good condition are a prerequisite because this is a minimally developed park.*

The landscape that embraces the ruins of Chaco Canyon appears almost lunar in its sterility.

The remains of Chaco Canyon appear almost as ancient and timeless as the colorful canyon walls that shelter them.

The sprawling remnants of Chaco Canyon reflect the gifted engineering prowess of this ghost city's creators and the ingenuity of those who once called this place home.

connect the settlements in the canyon with outlying pueblos, and even greater mysteries that await answers uncovered.

Although there are a number of never-to-be-forgotten sites in Chaco Canyon, Pueblo Bonito truly entrances. The three-acre, D-shaped structure was five stories at the back by the canyon wall and one story at the front facing the valley and contained approximately 650 large rooms around a plaza. As beautiful as the stonework is today, it must have been truly dazzling in appearance when it was covered with plaster and paint.

# CABEZON

Cabezon, named for the 7,785-foot basaltic volcanic plug that dominates the landscape around this quaint little ghost town, was never a hot bed of activity. Even at its prime in 1915, when the population topped three hundred, the town resembled a movie set caricature of the quintessential sleepy Mexican village circa 1850.

The desert meadows were a source of contention between the Navajo and the Apache before Spanish colonists began ranching and farming in this small valley along the Rio Puerco in 1767. The small colony fueled these confrontations, and both tribes suffered countless attacks until Kit Carson forced the Navajo to surrender in 1863.

Water was the second problem that confronted the settlers who farmed and raised sheep. The Rio Puerco dried to a muddy trickle during the summer, while winter and spring storms caused it to rage.

Still the hardy residents persisted and a dependable supply of water was established through a series of small dams. The community enjoyed a slow but steady

The unadorned simplicity of Cabezon in New Mexico's Rio Puerco Valley stands in contrast to the multihued hills and mountains than dominate the horizon.

growth, for a short time was an important stage stop on the road between Santa Fe and Fort Wingate, and supported a variety of small businesses as well as a school. Yet with the passing of each year, Cabezon became more and more a time capsule from another era.

A series of floods devastated many of the dams in the 1930s and was the first blow. Then, in the late 1940s, another series of floods hit the community, and then the river went dry.

With less than a whimper, the residents moved away. As with many western towns, the elements and vandals began to take their toll. Then something truly unique took place. An elderly man purchased much of the town site and appointed himself caretaker and guardian. As a result, access is very limited today, although visitors can see a great deal from the fence line.

In 1992, the Sandovals, a family that lives nearby in the circa-1872 stage station, began to restore the venerable old church. Since the restoration was completed, three special masses, followed by a potluck social, are held in the old church annually. More than fifty people are usually in attendance at each gathering.

## WHEN YOU GO

From Albuquerque, drive north 18 miles on Interstate 25 to exit 24 and turn west on U.S. Highway 550. Continue down U.S. 550 for 45 miles. Turn south onto the gravel access road leading to Cabezon and drive about 12 miles to the town.

# ABIQUIU

The lush pasturelands along the Rio Chama attracted Spanish colonists to the area in 1734. The colonists were not the first to settle in the small valley, as evidenced by the nearby ruins of an Indian pueblo. The settlement, then named Santa Rosa de Lima de Abiquiu, marked the northernmost point of colonization in 1734, and it suffered from near constant attack by Navajo, Apache, and Ute tribes.

These attacks severed the tenuous link with Santa Fe and forced the settlers to abandon the village. In 1750, under order of Governor Tomas Velez Cachupin, settlers returned to the site of the village and began reconstruction. A dozen Genizaros—Native Americans who had adopted Spanish customs and culture—accompanied the group.

The Genizaros occupied the bottom rung of social hierarchy in the Spanish colonies, but they received title to lands in exchange for settlement on the frontiers in an effort to establish buffer zones. In 1754, the Genizaros left the safety of the re-established community and moved three miles upriver to the site of the old pueblo and founded a more tolerant community that soon became a haven for settlers at a social disadvantage in Taos or Santa Fe.

The weathered adobe walls of Abiquiu stand as silent reminders that only the winds and sands are timeless.

With a history that spans centuries, Abiquiu is home to ruins that appear almost as ancient as the land itself.

Santa Rosa was a memory by 1793, but Abiquiu, the name bestowed upon the community founded on tolerance with the old pueblo as its foundation, flourished. The census that year showed a population of 1,363, which made it the third largest community in New Mexico.

It was also a prosperous community because its location and cultural diversity made it a key trading center for Native Americans throughout the region. In 1829, the community received a huge boost in prominence when Antonio Armijo designated it as the eastern terminus of the Spanish Trail that connected the colony of New Mexico with the San Gabriel Mission near Los Angeles. In 1852, the village became the base of operation for the U.S. Army in an effort to subdue the Navajo, Ute, and Jicarilla Apache tribes.

With the subjection of area tribes, the town became a quiet farming community and rapidly faded in prominence. It remained a small, sleepy forgotten village for almost a century. Today, one of the primary attractions in Abiquiu is the home of iconic artist Georgia O'Keeffe. Other sights include a wide array of old adobes, the mosque that is part of the Muslim retreat center built in the 1980s, and the beautiful scenery.

## WHEN YOU GO

*Abiquiu is located 48 miles north of Santa Fe on U.S. Highway 84.*

# ELIZABETHTOWN

From almost any place in the Moreno Valley, the 12,441-foot summit of Mount Baldy dominates the landscape. The sparse ruins of Elizabethtown are haunting and awe-inspiring against this backdrop.

It was near the summit of this towering peak that Captain William Moore, a sutler at nearby Fort Union, and William Kroenig opened the Mystic copper mine in 1866. Their discovery of gold in nearby Willow Creek the following spring soon eclipsed their promising mine and sparked the rush that created Elizabethtown.

Moore and Kroenig quickly capitalized on the influx of prospectors to the valley by opening a store and sawmill. By 1868, a town, named after Moore's daughter, Elizabeth, had risen around their new enterprise. She resided in the community until her death in 1934.

Elizabethtown became the first incorporated community in New Mexico in 1869. That year the editor of the *Santa Fe Gazette* noted, "There is considerable bustle and business in the air to be seen, and especially should you go into Abor's Saloon, you will be convinced that this is a stirring place. There are several stores,

Winter comes early and stays late in the high mountains around Elizabethtown, so structures are built with solid stone or logs.

A weathered barn and modern teepee hint that there is still a pulse in Elizabethtown, where some folks still call this former boomtown home.

two restaurants, and many saloons, as also a drug store, a billiard table, a barber shop, and gambling houses where a miner can deposit all his hard earned earnings of weeks in a few hours."

Fine dining was available at the hotel owned by Henry Lambert, a former cook for President Abraham Lincoln. Lambert relocated to Cimarron in the fall of 1871 and opened the St. James Hotel. Among the celebrities that frequented the town were Black Jack Ketchum and Clay Allison, although they were known for their dubious character.

Placer mining and lode mines fueled steady growth, even though the town nestled high in the Sangre de Cristo Mountains suffered from a chronic water shortage. To rectify this problem, in the summer of 1869, Moore and several other miners formed a partnership to channel the waters from near the headwaters of the Red River to the placer operations and town. The resulting forty-mile system

of aqueduct and ditches was amazing. The projected flow was less than antici-
pated, so efforts to tap the waters of Moreno Creek and the Ponil River followed.

Mayhem was a way of life in frontier mining camps, and Elizabethtown was
no exception. One incident, however, was so heinous that even the most hardened
folks were shocked. A lack of suitable lodging, especially during the harsh months
of winter, made operating a hostel a profitable venture. Charles Kennedy had capitalized on the largely transient population by killing lodgers, dismembering the
bodies for burning or burial in the cellar, and pocketing the valuables. He met his
fate at the hands of local vigilantes.

Two quick blows led to a rapid wane in Elizabethtown's prominence: the exhaustion of many ore bodies and placer fields, and the increasingly dominant role
of nearby Cimarron on the Santa Fe Trail. By 1875, the town had plummeted in
population from several thousand to several hundred.

The town enjoyed a brief but small renaissance in 1901 when a mining
company dammed the small Moreno River and began dredging operations. The
endeavor initially proved to be quite profitable, but by 1904, the operation was
suspended and Elizabethtown faded into obscurity.

Today the town consists of mine tailings, picturesque ruins, and a small museum located in a former schoolteacher's home that is framed by majestic views.
The deep snows of winter make summer the best time for visiting the site.

## WHEN YOU GO

*From Cimarron, drive 23 miles west on U.S. Highway 64, and continue north
for 5 miles on State Highway 38.*

With a little imagination, it seems as though laughter and music can be heard in the cool winds that whistle among the ruins.

# MADRID

Madrid, as with many frontier-era communities in the Southwest, is rooted in the discovery of gold and silver. However, Madrid is unusual because the mines that kept it alive through 1954 never produced one ounce of the precious yellow metal or silver.

Native Americans mined turquoise about five miles north of Madrid for centuries before the Spanish began mining silver and lead with the help of Native American slave labor at Los Cerrillos. After the Pueblo Revolt of 1680, the mining of silver and lead from these hills was sporadic until the mid-1850s when mining began in earnest.

Several large discoveries sparked a boom in the 1870s, and the camp, renamed Cerrilos, soon became an orderly settlement of laid out streets and established districts. Ample amounts of coal used for heat during the cold winter months were among the many luxuries enjoyed by Cerillos residents.

The construction of a southern transcontinental rail line reached Cerrilos in 1880, and the coalfields to the south became a commodity almost as valuable as gold or silver. A rare geologic anomaly resulted in anthracite, and the presence of bituminous coal in the area added to the field's importance.

Madrid, New Mexico, stretches the definition of ghost town, as it is home to dozens of residents, a vital artist community, and numerous surviving structures.

The Old Boarding House Mercantile in Madrid exemplifies the historic coal-mining town's rebirth as an artist colony in recent years.

In addition to developing the coal mines, the railroad also established Madrid by importing company houses from Kansas and reassembling them on site, and it built a spur line from Cerrilos. By 1900, the mines were running three shifts, and the town boasted a population of twenty-five hundred.

In 1906, the railroad leased the entire Madrid operation to the Colorado Fuel & Iron Company. This enterprise didn't last long after a major fire in one of the tunnels forced mining to completely stop. In an instant, the residents of Madrid faced community abandonment and no source of income.

The crisis passed quickly when the Hahn Coal Company in Albuquerque acquired the mines and town and initiated operations with the most modern equipment and methods. Under the leadership of Superintendent Oscar Huber, the town blossomed from a sooty, dreary company town into a showplace. Flower boxes added color to bland row houses, the water supply became consistent, pavement alleviated the dust on the main street, miners and their families had access to the hospital for three dollars per month, and electricity provided to employees at no charge eliminated the danger of fire that had plagued the community for years. Organization of an employee's club provided a wide array of recreational

Large sections of Madrid's former residential district still reflect its glory days, abandonment, and years of decline.

Easy access, friendly residents, and an extensive number of remaining buildings make Madrid an excellent introduction for the novice ghost town explorer.

opportunities, and the company paid for transportation when the town's baseball team was on the road.

All of these transformations paled in comparison to Huber's efforts to bring the community together during Christmas. The first holiday after the town was wired for electricity, Huber commissioned the construction of huge, lighted nativity figures as an illuminated Bethlehem on the hill above town.

The display grew larger every year until colorful biblical scenes covered both sides of the canyon and colorful lights shone brightly on most houses and businesses. Choral groups strategically placed throughout the town performed every evening during the week before Christmas. Visitors from as far away as Albuquerque made the pilgrimage to see the spectacle.

As natural gas replaced coal to heat homes and locomotives switched from steam to diesel, the demand for coal declined, the mines curtailed their production. In mid-1954, the mines closed. Within weeks, Madrid became a ghost town and home to four families.

In the mid-1970s, Oscar's son, Joe, decided to revive the town by offering the old houses for pennies on the dollar. The efforts were successful in the sense that today Madrid is a small art community with a café, museum, and colorful history.

## WHEN YOU GO

*Madrid is located 30 miles south of Santa Fe on State Highway 14.*

# GHOSTS OF CENTRAL NEW MEXICO

BILLY THE KID, THE FIRST CONTROLLED ATOMIC BLAST, AN ANCIENT CITY, AND SPANISH conquistadors are all threads in the colorful tapestry that is central New Mexico. The tangible links to this rich cornucopia of history abound here in the ghost towns, as well as along the roads that lead to them.

Small detours from the road to Gran Quivira lead to the wonders of the Manzano Mountains State Park and the Cibola National Forest. The beautiful Valley of Fires Recreation Area is found near White Oaks. Short detours on the roads to Lincoln provide access to the site of Fort Stanton and Ruidoso Museum of the Horse.

The diversity of central New Mexico landscapes is nothing short of astounding. The dramatic changes in elevation make it feasible to plan a trip for any season of the year.

Also, all of the towns featured in this chapter are accessible by automobile.

The kiva in Gran Quivira, as in other Native American communities of the time, was the religious center for the community.

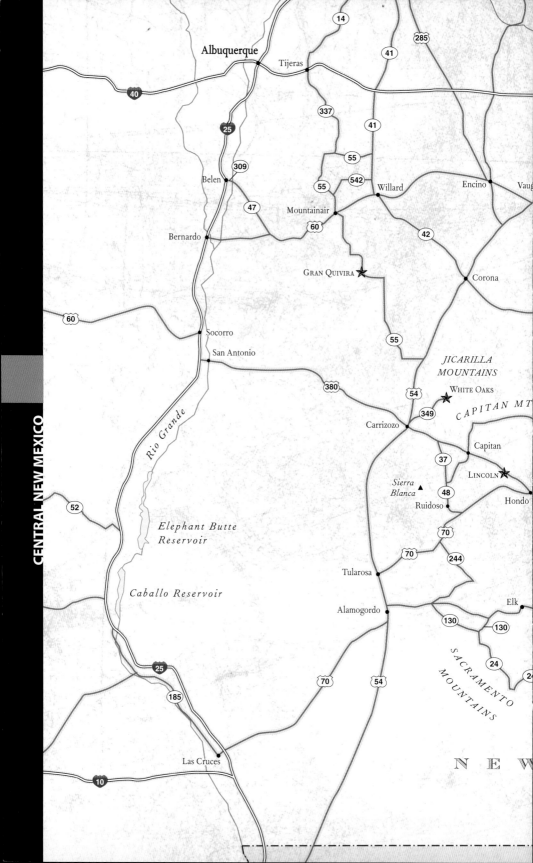

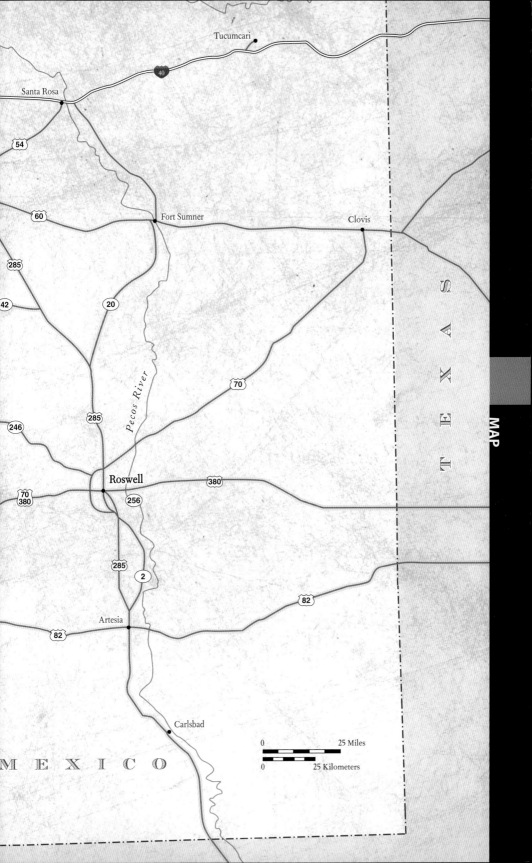

# GRAN QUIVIRA

The piles of limestone that were once towering walls and the rolling, open plains of the Estancia Valley that sweep to the horizon in all directions present a forlorn picture. They are the remains of Gran Quivira, which was the largest pueblo mission and the southernmost village of those that compose the Salinas Pueblo Missions National Monument.

When Don Juan de Onate arrived in the area during the fall of 1598, the three hundred–year-old village called Cueloze was a vital trading hub with a population estimated at two thousand. The explorers were amazed by the sophistication of the community, the wide array of goods being traded, and the stripes painted across the nose of residents, which led Spanish explorers to dub the village Pueblo de las Humanas.

Fray Francisco Letrado accepted the assignment of resident priest in 1629 and initiated construction of the village's first mission church. The church was

The austere landscapes that surround Gran Quivira today stretch the most fertile imagination when trying to see this as a rich agricultural area in central New Mexico.

*Top and bottom:* The expansive array of stone ruins at Gran Quivira is proof that this was once a solid, bustling, and modern community at the heart of a vast trading empire.

The finely crafted stone walls that stretch toward the sky offer mute testimony of the skills and craftsmanship of the Tompiro Indians who built Gran Quivira.

finished in 1634 and featured thirty-foot-high, white plaster walls and decorative red and black ornamentation, which stood in contrast to the rough natural stone construction of the rest of the village.

The social disruptions, coupled with diseases brought by the Spanish and a severe drought that began in the late 1660s, devastated the entire valley and led to extensive starvation and an exodus from the area villages, including Gran Quivira. By 1672, the wind and wildlife were the sole occupants of the once vibrant village. The ruins of the community, as well as those of Abo and Quarai, are now part of the Salinas Pueblo Missions National Monument that is administered by the U.S. National Park Service. Each pueblo has a visitor center and exhibits.

## WHEN YOU GO

*From Mountainair, drive south 26 miles on State Highway 55.*

# WHITE OAKS

The founding of White Oaks is the quintessential western mining camp story, at least according to legend. Four prospectors working their way through the Jicarilla Mountains in 1879 discovered a fabulously rich outcropping of gold ore in a quartz vein along the eastern slope of Baxter Mountain. One of the prospectors, a wanted fugitive, sold his share in the claim for a pony, bottle of whiskey, and forty dollars when it appeared the vein was merely an anomaly. The others stuck it out, and the North Homestake Mine soon became one of the largest producers in the territory.

Whatever the origin of White Oaks may be, within three years a town had mushroomed in the shadow of Baxter Mountain, and miners pulled astounding loads of profitable ores from mines such as the Lady Godiva, Rip van Winkle, and Boston Boy. As a historical footnote, the town's Old Abe Mine was the deepest dry shaft in the world at 1,375 feet.

Watson Hoyle, operations supervisor at the Old Abe, built an intricate Victorian-styled edifice that is still a source of pride for the old mining town. A beautiful brick schoolhouse on a hill above town, an opera house, a church,

The 1893 Brown Store that once served as the jail in White Oaks gets a new lease on life thanks to an extensive renovation.

*Above and next spread:* The school in White Oaks served its original purpose from 1895 to 1947. It was a community center in the years that followed the school's closure.

*Opposite:* Since 1887, the towering Hoyle House, built at a reputed cost of forty thousand dollars, has been a landmark in White Oaks.

A doorless safe in White Oaks fuels the imagination as to what role it played in the history of this colorful mining camp.

a bank, saloons, and a newspaper contributed to the establishment of the largest community in Lincoln County.

Celebrities associated with White Oaks include Billy the Kid; Susan McSween-Barber, the "Cattle Queen of New Mexico"; and Madame Varnish, proprietor of the local casino that dispensed other forms of entertainment. Perhaps the most notable was William McDonald, a local attorney who later served as the first governor of New Mexico.

Two blows struck the community in 1897: the depletion of primary gold deposits and the rerouting of a planned railroad. By the turn of the century, the town had settled into a state of slumber that persists to this day. A surprising number of original buildings are still here, and no visit to White Oaks is complete without a stop at the Cedarvale Cemetery.

## WHEN YOU GO

*From Carrizozo, drive north on U.S. Highway 54 for 4 miles to State Highway 349. Continue on Highway 349 for 5 miles to White Oaks.*

The number of stars in the flag in front of the old law offices in White Oaks provide a clue this photo was not taken in 1890.

# LINCOLN

Only Tombstone enjoys more notoriety in western history and lore than the ghost town of Lincoln, which is situated in the lovely Rio Bonito Valley. Lincoln, unlike Tombstone, is preserved in its entirety as a national historic landmark.

The origins of this charming community date to the mid-1850s, shortly after the Mexican-American War, when displaced Mexicans began farming in this valley and established the village of La Placita del Rio Bonito, which translates to the Little Village by the Pretty River. The centerpiece of the new village was a round, brick fortification to provide protection from Apache raiders.

With the establishment of Fort Stanton a few miles to the west in 1855, the valley entered an era of tranquility and prosperity. The next transitional milestone for the community was in 1869 when the territorial legislature approved the creation of Lincoln County and the town was renamed Lincoln and appointed as the county seat.

Lincoln, New Mexico, has been preserved in such an original state that Billy the Kid could still find his way around town if he were to return today.

Lincoln is a bona fide time capsule of frontier life in the New Mexico Territory.

The feeling of utopia ended in 1878 after a five-day gun battle marked the culmination of the Lincoln County War, which established the town's violent reputation. Vestiges from that bloody spring abound in Lincoln.

Casa de Patron was built by Juan Patron in the mid-1860s. It served as his home and a store. Billy the Kid was held under house arrest at the Casa de Patron after he was convicted in Mesilla for killing Sheriff Bill Brady. The Montano Store next door has an extensive display on the town's history.

The Ellis Store also survives as a bed and breakfast. The store served as the headquarters for the Regulators, an armed gang formed to avenge the murder of John Tunstall. Billy the Kid was among the gang's members. More than a thousand items of original inventory at the Tunstall Store are still on display, and this also is the headquarters for the Lincoln State Monument.

Additional time capsules include the Lincoln County Courthouse, originally the Murphy-Dolan Store, from which Billy the Kid escaped in the spring of 1881; the 1921 adobe school, now an art gallery; and the Wortley Hotel built in 1881.

TORREON
One of Lincoln's earliest structures. Built in the 1850's, its thick walls protected Spanish-Americans against the Apaches. In Lincoln Co. War Murphy's sharpshooters were here stationed. In 1937 Chaves County Historical Society undertook restoration of tower.

The Torreon Tower dates to the 1850s and was built for defense against marauding Apache warriors. It is one of the oldest structures in Lincoln.

The Tunstall-McSween Store in Lincoln is a true Old West throwback because much of the inventory dates to the time when Billy the Kid stood in this store.

There are no souvenir shops here, only a package of historic buildings that leave the town looking as it did during the tumultuous days of the Lincoln County War. A walking tour that begins at the Anderson-Freeman Visitor's Center and Museum is the best way to experience this rare gem.

## WHEN YOU GO

*From Roswell, drive east for 47 miles on U.S. Highway 70. At the junction of U.S. 70 and U.S. Highway 380, turn onto U.S. 380 and continue 6 miles.*

By the 1870s, the Hispanic population of Lincoln County had become serfs to the business monopoly of James Dolan and L. G. Murphy, who operated under the questionable legal umbrella of Thomas Catron, a Santa Fe–based lawyer. When a former employee and ambitious young attorney by the name of Alexander McSween joined forces with John Chisum, a prominent local rancher, and John Tunstall, a successful businessman, the Dolan/Murphy contingent turned to guns to maintain their lucrative enterprise.

The tensions between the factions continued to build until Sheriff Bill Brady, who was under control of the Dolan/Murphy machine, and a posse arrived at Tunstall's ranch to collect on a trumped up debt owed to McSween, who had stored valuable goods at the ranch. It is unknown what exactly transpired that January day in 1878, but the shooting death of Tunstall was the spark that transformed a feud into a war.

The final showdown of an event, now known as the Lincoln County War, took place on April 1, 1878, when Billy the Kid, an employee of Tunstall, and four other gunmen ambushed Sheriff Brady as he attempted to serve McSween with a warrant. The gang fled into the nearby hills, and the Kid and McSween returned to town with more than forty hired guns and took cover in the Montano Store and the McSween house next to Tunstall's store.

Both sides exchanged gunfire for the next five days until a contingent of soldiers arrived from Fort Stanton with a howitzer and Gatling gun. The McSween home was torched, and the fire forced those holed up there to flee. In the running gun battle that ensued, the Kid escaped into the night, McSween was mortally wounded, and several others were killed.

# GHOSTS OF SOUTHWEST NEW MEXICO

SOME OF THE MOST EXCITING AND MOST OVERLOOKED GHOST TOWNS in the Southwest are hidden among the national forests, wilderness areas, and stark desert plains of western New Mexico. Many of these are also the most easily accessible ghost towns in the area.

The towns that survive are connected by pivotal events in history, as well as legendary figures, and serve as dusty reminders of when the area was the frontier. Framed by majestic scenery, the towns are also a photographer's paradise.

Empty doorways and windows frame the stunning western landscapes, horizons, and quickly vanishing remnants from Riley, New Mexico.

In Chloride, an old adobe teeters between the past and present, between collapse and still providing shelter for those who call this town home.

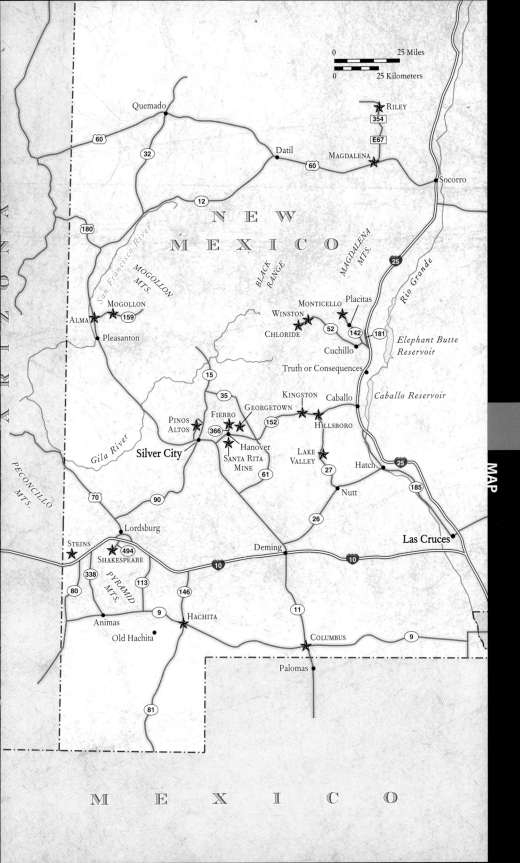

# RILEY

The skyline of hills and buttes above Riley on the north bank of the Rio Salado is unchanged from 1880, when construction began on the first buildings in the town then known as Santa Rita. The only thing that has changed is the landscape.

The high deserts that surround the town site today make it difficult to imagine this was once a prosperous farming community. It is even harder to envision the Rio Salado as anything more than a ribbon of sand after the water table dropped in the late 1920s.

The town enjoyed relative prosperity and slow but steady growth throughout the closing years of the nineteenth century. The approval for a post office under the name of Riley came in 1890.

The sizable discovery of coal and manganese in the nearby hills sparked a small mining boom in 1897. By the turn of the century, the simple adobes of Riley's 150 residents stretched along the banks of the Rio Salado and to the hills behind the stone-built school, one of the town's two remaining structures. The

other is the church, which is maintained by a caretaker and where mass is held every May on the feast day of the town's patron saint, Santa Rita.

The remnants of the town, which consist of scattered foundations and extensive adobe ruins, are found throughout the scenic location.

In Riley, the extensive adobe ruins and cold industrial relics of mining are disappearing in the harsh high desert climate of western New Mexico.

## WHEN YOU GO

*From Magdalena, drive north on County Road E67, which becomes Forest Road 354, for 20 miles. Four-wheel drive is not needed, but ground clearance is very important. You should inquire about the road conditions in Magdalena before your trip, and park on the south side of the river and cross the Rio Salado on foot.*

# MAGDALENA

The small camp of Kelly sprang to life in 1864 after the discovery of lead and silver in the foothills of the Magdalena Mountains. The rugged terrain and deep canyons prevented extensive growth of the camp, so another community, Magdalena, was established a couple of miles to the north.

Magdalena served as a supply and recreation center for the mines at Kelly and the burgeoning ranching industry that was developing on the plains of San Augustin. Not surprisingly, it was a rough-and-tumble town with a disproportionate number of saloons.

In the early 1880s, Gustav Billing, owner of the smelter in Socorro, purchased the Kelly Mine. Rather than continue the laborious and expensive transport of ore thirty miles to Socorro by mule, he initiated an agreement with the Atchison, Topeka & Santa Fe Railroad for construction of a spur line to Magdalena.

After the line was completed in January 1885, Magdalena soon became a prosperous and respectable community with a promising future. Within twelve months,

The towering edifices of the Kelly Mine have dominated the New Mexico landscape for more than a century.

the population soared to almost two thousand, and the business district included several stores, livery stables, saloons, a boarding house, and a blacksmith shop.

Magdalena became an important shipping point for livestock. In 1916, the Department of the Interior restricted homesteading in west-central New Mexico and opened 71,000 acres as a thoroughfare for ranchers in eastern Arizona and on the plains of San Augustin to drive cattle and sheep along the Magdalena Stock Driveway. Today U.S. Highway 60 largely follows this route.

After the corridor was established, ranching and Magdalena boomed. In 1920, Magdalena was second only to Chicago in the number of livestock shipped by rail, according to the U.S. National Park Service.

In the late 1890s, production from the mines at Kelly slowed after the primary ore bodies were exhausted. It ramped up again when it was discovered that the green rocks tossed aside as waste for almost forty years were a rare and valuable zinc carbonate. In 1904, the Sherwin-Williams paint company bought the Graphic Mine, and the Tri-State Bullion Smelting and Development Company purchased the Kelly Mine and built a smelter on site.

Zinc production reached its peak in 1928, and the mines closed shortly after. Ranchers continued to utilize the railhead at Magdalena through the 1960s, although trucks had replaced the stock driveway by the mid-1930s. The rail spur closed in 1971, and the only things that kept the town alive were the tourists and sportsmen traveling on U.S. 60.

Today Magdalena is relatively quiet town with a wide array of buildings, ruins, and homes that represent more than a century of history. These, along with the picturesque setting, make this a delightful place to explore with a camera in hand.

## WHEN YOU GO

*From Socorro, drive west 27 miles on U.S. Highway 60 to Magdalena.*

Reflecting golden sun, the sign at the entrance to the Kelly Mine property hints that these abandoned buildings once were the heart of an empire.

# MONTICELLO, CHLORIDE, AND WINSTON

The towns of Winston and Chloride, and to a lesser degree Placitas and Monticello, are among the rare survivors of the Black Range boom. These beautiful, forested, well-watered mountains and canyons were the home of the Apache who fought to maintain their hold until the early 1880s. Initially farming and ranching lured intrepid pioneers to attempt to gain control of the area. The promise of mineral riches was the motivation in later years.

The initial settlement of Placitas began in the 1840s. It was situated along Alamosa Creek at the southern end of Monticello Canyon. The little village developed into a quiet little farming community in spite of sporadic raids by the Apache. American influences increased with each passing year and took root farther up the canyon with the establishment of Canada Alamosa in 1856 and renamed Monticello in 1881.

Monticello was in actuality a small square fortification for protection against raids. However, as with its neighbor to the south, the town settled into peaceful stability over time. Placitas and Monticello maintain small populations and have active churches (the one in Monticello dates to 1908), but picturesque ruins, such as the 1930s-era, WPA-built school in Monticello, attest to better times. Both towns are located along the Geronimo Trail Scenic Byway.

Chloride and Winston are a few miles to the west as the crow flies and located on the west side of the Sierra Cuchillo Mountains. These towns were the antithesis of their neighbors in that they were rowdy mining camps. Their needs fueled the prosperity of Monticello and Placitas.

The settlement that eventually became Chloride was founded by Harry Pye, a muleskinner by trade who had dreams of being a successful prospector. He discovered a rich deposit of silver along Mineral Creek while hauling supplies from Hillsboro to the army encamped at Ojo Caliente during the spring of 1879.

Pye patiently fulfilled his military contract and returned in 1881 to file a claim. As word of the discovery spread, miners, prospectors, and those who prospered from their success flooded the area in spite of the infringement on Apache lands and subsequent reprisals.

For more than a century, this old church has served the community of Monticello and is still the centerpiece of life in this remote mountain mining camp.

The ruins of the Works Projects Administration–built school in Monticello, New Mexico, hint of better times in this forgotten mining town.

Rusting relics of the modern era blend seamlessly with traces of the frontier era under cinematic western skies in Monticello.

The settlement originally known as Pyetown officially became Chloride with the establishment of a post office. The town's name indicated what the ore found there was composed of. By the late 1880s, the town consisted of more than one hundred homes; numerous stores, including a butcher shop and candy store; an attorney's office; a doctor's office; a Chinese laundry; a hotel; a boarding house; a stage line that connected the mountain community with towns to the south; and a newspaper.

In the modern vernacular, Winston would be called a suburb of Chloride, although Winston's population dwarfed its neighbor for a brief time in the late nineteenth century. Winston was originally called Fairview, but its name was changed to honor Frank Winston, a successful prospector turned businessman who was also a philanthropist in the remote mountain mining camps.

The financial Panic of 1893 fueled a collapse of silver prices and would have destroyed both communities if it had not been for the fortuitous discovery of rich copper, lead, and zinc deposits. This find kept both frontier-era mining camps alive into the modern era.

Winston's downward slump was slow and began with closure of Chloride's mines in the early 1930s. By 1940, the population was around several hundred, down from a peak of several thousand. Today the population is near the single digits, yet the town consists of more than thirty buildings.

Monticello is not a true ghost, as a number of folks still call it home and dwell in its historic structures.

Chloride's main street has few hints indicating this isolated community was once the gem of the Black Range.

Forlorn markers and classic western vistas give Chloride a haunting solitude and sense of eternity.

Spared the destruction wrought by vandals in more isolated mining camps, Chloride's picturesque ruins make it the quintessential ghost town.

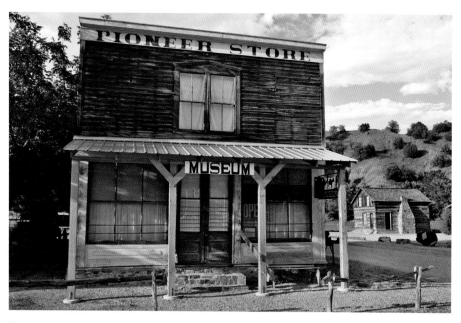
The Pioneer Store in Chloride, New Mexico, still has an original inventory that dates to the 1920s.

Chloride's decline largely mirrored Winston's. The log-constructed Pioneer Store that was built in 1880 was "temporarily" closed in 1923. More than sixty years later, Don Edmund, whose family has saved numerous structures in Chloride, purchased the store in 1989 and was surprised to find a large percentage of the inventory remained.

All four of these towns are well worth the effort to seek them out. The communities are easily accessed, except after snowstorms in the winter.

## WHEN YOU GO

*From Truth or Consequences, drive north on Interstate 25 to exit 83. Then drive north on State Highway 181 for 5 miles, and turn west on State Highway 52. The drive to Winston is 27 miles, and Chloride is 2.5 miles farther to the west. Placitas is located 24 miles from Truth or Consequences. Follow the directions to Winston/Chloride, but after driving 5 miles on Highway 52, turn north on State Highway 142.*

# HILLSBORO AND KINGSTON

Dan Dugan and Dave Stitzel were winding up another fruitless prospecting venture in the early spring of 1877 when they set up camp on the banks of Percha Creek on the eastern flanks of the Black Mountains. What they thought to be useless float turned out to be gold.

Before summer turned to fall, the rolling hills that surrounded the initial claims were swarming with prospectors, numerous mines were expanding at astounding rates, and a small, boisterous community was quickly forming along the creek. The legend is that the town of Hillsborough, later spelled Hillsboro, was chosen by drawing the suggestion from a hat.

Hillsboro was well on its way to becoming a small metropolis in the wilderness when another ore discovery was made seven miles to the west in 1882. This strike was so rich that a single piece of float exhibited in Denver sparked a boom so large that a town materialized at the site within weeks.

Soon Hillsboro and Kingston became known as the "Gems of the Black Range." This area was the most productive and profitable mining district in the territory with the discovery of silver at nearby Lake Valley in 1876. Although both communities began as a collection of rough-and-tumble canvas-topped wood shacks, they were modern, substantial towns by 1890. The population in the two communities was estimated at seven thousand before the close of the century.

Kingston reportedly consisted of more than twenty saloons, including Pretty Sam's Casino & Dance Hall (a bed and breakfast was built from the ruins), a church, a school, stores, and a bank. The majority of the buildings were built from locally quarried stone. In 1884, the territorial legislature created Sierra County from portions of Grant, Socorro, and Dona Ana counties, and Hillsboro was designated as the county seat.

The courthouse was built of red brick on the hill above town and reflected the importance of the community. It was also center stage for one of the most important trials held during the closing years of the nineteenth century in the New Mexico Territory. The sensational murder case of Albert Fountain and his son remains unsolved.

Many colorful characters lived in western frontier towns, and J. W. and Sadie Orchard were two interesting Hillsboro residents. This amazing couple operated

The Percha Bank in Kingston, New Mexico, is among the few surviving vestiges from when this raucous mining town was a center of commerce in the Black Mountains.

Albert Fountain arrived in New Mexico during 1862 with the Union Army's California Column. He was fascinated by the territory, and he opened a law office in Messila after the war. His standing in that community, enhanced by marrying into a prominent Mexican family, rose quickly and led to the founding of *The Republican* newspaper.

Fountain's fearless reputation for challenging corruption at all levels led the Southeastern New Mexico Stock Growers Association to enlist his services to investigate cattle rustling charges against Oliver Lee in mid-1895. Lee was a relative latecomer to the Tularosa Valley, but his herds expanded at such a prodigious rate that many felt his holdings included cattle from other ranches.

Fountain traveled to Lincoln, with his eight-year-old son, to secure indictments for larceny of cattle against Lee in late January 1896. Fountain and his son, Henry, left Lincoln on February 1 with the indictments, but they never arrived in Messila.

Dona Ana County Sheriff Pat Garrett, who was famous for shooting Billy the Kid, spent two years investigating the disappearance and even offered a ten thousand dollar reward for information before he charged Lee and James Gilland, a ranch hand, with murder. The trial venue moved to Sierra County because passions involving the case were running so high in the area.

The Hillsboro courthouse was filled with spectators during the three-week trial. The jury deliberated a mere eight minutes before reaching a verdict of not guilty. More than a century after the disappearance of Fountain and his son, the location of the bodies and the circumstances of their disappearance remain a mystery.

a successful stage line from Silver City during the height of the Apache wars. In the late 1880s, they added a line from Hillsboro to Kingston that went on to Lake Valley and then to the railroad at Nutt. London-born Sadie was often at the reins of the six-horse team that pulled the heavy Concord coaches through the daunting terrain.

A number of structures remain in Hillsboro and Kingston because red brick, stone, and adobe were the primary materials of choice in both communities. The long list of photographic delights include the Percha Bank in Kingston and the courthouse and jail ruins that loom above Hillsboro. Other must-see sites are the Black Range Museum and the general store in Hillsboro. The store's doors opened in 1879, and it is now one of the oldest continuously operated stores in the state.

## WHEN YOU GO

*From Caballo, take exit 63 off I-25. Turn west on State Highway 152 and drive 17 miles to Hillsboro. Kingston is 7 miles farther west on Highway 152.*

# LAKE VALLEY

Death and gun smoke transformed Lincoln and Tombstone from dusty frontier towns to icons of the Old West. Silver, the richest deposit ever discovered, elevated Lake Valley from a sleepy little stage station to a bustling well-to-do community.

The legend of the storied Bridal Chamber silver deposit begins in the summer of 1878 when George Lufkin, a cowboy and itinerant prospector, discovered a piece of rich float in an area near the small town of Lake Valley. The town at the time amounted to little more than a stage station and a scattering of cabins. Upon receipt of the assay report, Lufkin enlisted the aid of his friend, Chris Watson, and staked a claim.

Months passed, funds were exhausted, and in spite of promising leads, the two men had nothing to show for their efforts but several shallow shafts and a short tunnel. In what must have seemed a stroke of good luck, the Sierra Grande Mining Company, with financing from capitalists in Philadelphia, offered Lufkin and Watson one hundred thousand dollars for the claims.

Time stands still in Lake Valley, New Mexico. Many of the houses look as though the owner will soon return from a hard day in the mines.

Rusty relics from the golden age of Detroit without bullet holes are almost as scarce among the ghost towns of the Southwest as lost treasures.

## BRIDAL CHAMBER: EARLY FORTUNES, LATER DANGERS

The "Bridal Chamber" deposit, discovered in 1881, spurred mine development at Lake Valley.

In 1908, recalling the early days, Bernard MacDonald commented that the Bridal Chamber acquired its name "because of the sparkling light reflected by the myriads of crystals of cerargyrite and calcite studding the roof of the open space over the [silver] chloride streak."

Newspaper descriptions indicate this silver concentration was so rich that ore could be melted from the ceiling of the deposit using only the flame from a burning candle. One chunk of ore, called "Jackson's Baby" after the mine's manager, D.H. Jackson, was so large it had to be broken into pieces before it could be removed. Initial hopes of easy riches soon disappeared when this ore deposit was found to be unique and not duplicated anywhere else at Lake Valley.

Ore from the Bridal Chamber is reported to have yielded over 3.5 million ounces of silver before the deposit played out. In later years, the entrance to the Bridal Chamber collapsed, and the mine is now too dangerous to enter.

*Entrance of Bridal Chamber Mine, Lake Valley, New Mexico ca. 1890. Photo by H. A. Schmidt. Courtesy Palace of the Governors (Museum of New Mexico/DCA). Negative No.: 12655.*

LAKE VALLEY

A historic plaque at the fabled Bridal Chamber in Lake Valley, New Mexico, seems an austere monument to the richest silver strike in history.

The rocky monoliths of the Mimbres Mountains loom large above the sparse ruins, empty house, and barren desert plains of Lake Valley.

## WHEN YOU GO

*From Hillsboro, drive south 16 miles on State Highway 27.*

The new owner began leasing the claims in a fees-plus-percentage agreement. John Leavitt, a blacksmith in Lake Valley, began working the claim and within two days broke into a pocket of almost pure mineralization, which is a rare geologic anomaly. This was the Bridal Chamber, the richest silver discovery in history.

The walls of the small cavern were astonishingly pure. Legend is that some ore bypassed the smelter for direct shipment to the mint. In addition to the spur rail line from Nutt to the mill at Lake Valley, another line ran directly into the Bridal Chamber that records indicate hauled an astounding 2.5 million ounces of silver.

The Black Range Mining District—established in 1881 and dominated by Hillsboro, Kingston, and Lake Valley—became the richest-producing region in the territory. Saloons became the dominant business in Lake Valley, as was the case in most mining towns, but the community also supported numerous stores, blacksmith shops, boarding houses, and a church that garnered international acclaim for its funding of charitable work throughout the world.

Another treasure associated with Lake Valley is a gold stash that was hidden by Black Jack Ketchum. In 1892, Ketchum, his brother Sam, and several other outlaws held up a train at Nutt, a water stop north of Deming. A telegraph message sent to Lake Valley soon had a posse in hot pursuit as the bandits fled for Arizona. Legend has it that the outlaws, slowed by the weight of the gold, chose to stash it in the vicinity. The exact amount of money stolen and if it has ever been recovered remains a mystery to this day.

The exhaustion of the Bridal Chamber was the first blow to befall the community. The second and third came in rapid succession: the devaluing of silver in 1893 and a fire that devastated most of the business district in 1895. The town enjoyed a small resurrection for a brief period in the 1920s and again during World War II with the mining of manganese, but by 1954 the population had dwindled so much a post office could no longer be supported.

The slide to complete abandonment was a long one. The last service held in the church was in 1974, and twenty years later, the last resident passed away. Today the Bureau of Land Management maintains the town site. A caretaker is on site to provide information and direct a walking tour of the town with its extensive array of surviving structures.

# COLUMBUS

For a number of years, little differentiated Columbus, founded in 1891, from Palomas, Mexico, its neighbor directly across the border. Both were sleepy, dusty little backwater desert towns dependent on ranching. The construction of the El Paso & Southwestern Railroad that connected El Paso, Texas, with Douglas, Arizona, in 1902 brought many changes to Columbus. The first was the dismantling of the village and its reconstruction three miles to the north along the new rail line.

As a border city with rail access, Columbus gained an importance that belied its small size. In 1912, the U.S. Army chose Columbus as a site for a military base to monitor sixty-five miles of the United States/Mexico border, which was a need due to the concern about the Mexican revolution.

By 1915, Camp Furlong was a fully equipped base manned by a contingent of 350 soldiers of the Thirteenth Cavalry, and Columbus had grown to a population of 700. The business district consisted of several general stores, a depot, a Coca-Cola bottling works, three hotels, a bank, a drugstore, and a laundry.

A monument in Columbus, New Mexico, is one reminder that this tiny desert town was once at the center of an international crisis.

Because most of the troops chose to take their rest and recreation in Palomas, Columbus was a relatively orderly and quiet community.

In the early morning of March 9, 1916, the quiet was shattered, and Columbus was propelled into international headlines when several hundred Mexican revolutionaries under the leadership of General Francisco "Pancho" Villa stormed Columbus as a raiding party in search of supplies.

The residents of Columbus quickly found themselves in a large battle between soldiers, revolutionaries, and armed citizens. The unsuccessful raid lasted until dawn and left more than seventy revolutionaries and eighteen Americans dead.

Columbus was transformed into a smoking battlefield in less than two hours. Twenty-four hours later, it was a boomtown at the center of a rapidly expanding military encampment. Under orders from President Woodrow Wilson, and with permission from Mexican President Venustiano Carranza, General John J. "Black Jack" Pershing arrived in Columbus to lead a punitive military expedition into Mexico in pursuit of Pancho Villa. By March 10, Camp Furlong had an additional thousand troops, and within several months, the influx of military personnel had pushed Columbus to being the largest settlement in New Mexico.

With the expedition into Mexico from Columbus, the U.S. Army for the first time extensively utilized motorized vehicles, and this was one of the first times the army employed aircraft in its efforts. In fact, Columbus became the site of the first airfield built exclusively for military use in the United States.

Columbus began a slow spiral downward with the end of the Mexican campaign in early 1917 and the deactivation of Camp Furlong in 1926. The last train, the *Sunset Limited*, rolled through town in December 1961. The long slumber ended, to a degree, in the late 1970s when retirees discovered the quiet little town, and today the population has risen to almost seventeen hundred. The town's rediscovery has led to the preservation of a large number of historic buildings. Among the most notable are the El Paso & Southwestern Railroad Depot, built in 1902; the United States Custom House, built in 1902; and the Camp Furlong headquarters and recreation hall. Additional survivors from the infancy of Columbus and the time of the raid by Pancho Villa include the Hoover Hotel, the Camp Furlong court and jail, the elementary school, the town jail, and the ruins of the Rodriguez house with bullet holes in the walls with unverified claims that they were from the 1916 raid.

The Hoover Hotel on Broadway in Columbus, New Mexico, was ground zero during Pancho Villa's raid on this tiny railroad town.

This photo of Pancho Villa was taken before the raid on Columbus transformed a former Mexican presidential candidate into a wanted fugitive.

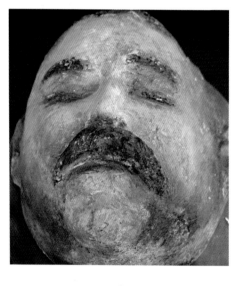

A copy of Pancho Villa's death mask is just one of the interesting exhibits at the museum in Columbus.

## WHEN YOU GO

*From Deming, drive 32 miles south on State Highway 11.*

# SHAKESPEARE

The foundation of the old adobe town of Shakespeare was a commodity more precious than gold in the desert: water. Yet when silver, gold, diamonds, and rubies were found in the area, Shakespeare became a boomtown.

In 1868, Jack Frost and John Everson, employees of the National Mail & Transportation Company, established a station at the north end of the Pyramid Mountains at one of the few dependable, year-round water holes in the desert. The Mexican Springs station was a desolate and lonely place for a short time.

The following year, prospectors discovered extensive silver deposits in the Burro Mountains to the north and small discoveries near Mexican Springs. Neither discovery would have been enough to launch a boom or transform Mexican Springs into a town if William C. Ralston, founder of the Bank of California, hadn't intervened.

Ralston saw great profit potential in the silver discovery. He began exaggerating the results of assay reports, leaking well-placed rumors, and funding his ventures with money from outside investors. He then acquired the property around Mexican Springs, which was occasionally referred to as Grant, laid out streets, sold lots, and renamed the settlement after himself.

The boom had busted by 1871, as the result of sparse returns from the mines and improperly filed claims. In the fall of 1872, two prospectors, Philip Arnold and John Slack, saved the town from complete abandonment with an amazing discovery of a vast field of diamonds and rubies.

The prospectors needed financial backing to develop the diamond mines and ventured to California to meet with the town's namesake. Ralston, excited by the discovery, was quite suspicious of the find. First, he had a sampling of the stones appraised. Then he hired a trusted mining engineer to evaluate the site. Then and only then did he offer to purchase the entire claim for a reputed six hundred thousand dollars. The scammer had been scammed.

Ralston replayed his highly profitable gambit from the silver mines, and the town of Ralston boomed larger than before. The population was estimated at three thousand by the following spring.

The diamond rush, as with the silver rush before it, was short-lived. The town was almost a complete ghost by 1875. The Bank of California collapsed that same year, and soon after the collapse, William Ralston drowned in San Francisco Bay, a rumored suicide.

A new era dawned in Ralston in April 1879 when English-born Colonel William G. Boyle, a mining engineer, and his brother, General John Boyle, purchased the town site and the primary silver mines discovered in 1870. The brothers created the Shakespeare Gold & Silver Mining Company, which led to changing Ralston's name to Shakespeare.

Main Street continued with the Shakespeare theme and was renamed Avon Avenue. The refurbished hotel became the Stratford on Avon.

Within a few years, the town was firmly rooted in real mine development and had grown to one hundred residents who supported several saloons, an assay office, and a general store. Among the luminaries to invest in and visit the small mining town was Lew Wallace, governor of the New Mexico Territory from 1878 to 1881 and author of the novel *Ben Hur*.

The mines at Shakespeare were in decline when the Panic of 1893 brought silver mining to a complete stop (there had been no discovery of gold in profitable

Diamond hoaxes, a mysterious California suicide, a Shakespearean remake, and connections with Lew Wallace, author of *Ben Hur*, make Shakespeare one of the unique ghost towns in the Southwest.

The Grant House is one of the oldest structures in Shakespeare and has served a number of functions, including as a stage station.

quantities). The final blow was in 1894 with the establishment of Lordsburg four miles to the north along the new Southern Pacific Railroad tracks.

Most of the businesses and residents of Shakespeare relocated to Lordsburg. A few others moved a few miles south to a new camp built around 85 Mine, a new and promising discovery.

Shakespeare waned so much that construction of a spur line run connecting Lordsburg to the 85 Mine ran right down the center of Avon Avenue in 1914.

The next chapter for Shakespeare began in 1935 when Frank and Rita Hill purchased a large section of acreage that included the ruins and town site for use as a ranch. They refurbished one of the original buildings as their home, other buildings received similar treatment as time allowed, and the town opened as a tourist attraction.

Rita published an interesting booklet for visitors that chronicled the town's history. To promote the ghost town as an attraction, Frank and his daughter, Janaloo, with extensive press coverage and numerous interviews given en route, rode horseback all the way to San Diego, California.

Today, Shakespeare is somewhere between re-created, resurrected, and pure ghost. The town is open on select weekends and by appointment. You can contact the owners by calling 505-531-2711.

## WHEN YOU GO

*From Lordsburg, drive south for 4 miles on State Highway 494.*

The owners of Shakespeare have gone to great lengths to ensure its visitors experience an immersion into life in the frontier era in the desert Southwest.

The re-creation in Shakespeare extends to the sparse furnishings that reflect the austerity of life in the Southwest's former remote mining communities.

# HACHITA

The historic consensus is that the naming of Hachita—derived from the Spanish word *hacha*, meaning small axe or hatchet—had to do with one of the many similarly named landmarks surrounding the Hachita Valley, such as Big Hatchet Peak and Little Hatchet Mountains. Why these geologic features received the moniker remains a mystery.

Since at least the 1860s, prospectors wandered these desert hills and found little to justify being attacked by the bands of Apaches who dominated the surrounding valleys. The discovery of sizable deposits of silver, copper, and gold in the early 1870s changed everything, and in the blink of an eye, the spotlight was on the Hachita Valley.

By 1877, several highly productive mines had been established, including the American National, the Hornet, and the King, which led the territorial legislature to designate this area as the Eureka Mining District. All frontier booms need a boomtown, and this one had Eureka, a rowdy, wild, untamed, dusty collection of tents, stone and adobe cabins, and dugouts.

Civility and civilization arrived when the Southern Pacific Railroad passed within forty-five miles of the community as construction progressed westward from El Paso. Eureka officially became Hachita with the establishment of a post office in 1882.

By the mid-1880s, the remote little town boasted a population of several hundred, a steam-powered mill, several saloons, a couple of general stores, and a small hotel. For a brief moment, it looked as though Hachita had a promising future. However, by 1890, the mines had played out, and the town became a ghost town with just enough people left to keep the post office open until 1898.

The desert was reclaiming Hachita when, in 1902, the El Paso & Southwestern Railroad built a line through the valley about seven miles to the east and a small camp was established at a siding to provide water for the engines. The proximity of the railroad spurred renewed interest in the mines at Hachita, which in turn transformed the railroad service camp into a small supply center for the mines and area ranches.

The application for a post office in Hachita in late 1902 caused a bit of confusion, but locals took to calling the original town Old Hachita.

An ocotillo on a rocky plain framing a tattered cabin under a panoramic sky in Old Hachita, New Mexico, is the romanticized view of the ghost town.

Collapsing mines in Old Hachita, as well as in most ghost towns throughout the Southwest, are a serious danger and should be avoided.

The simplistic sturdy nature of this small adobe chapel reflects the spirit of the second incarnation of Hachita.

As the new town grew, it began to mirror its namesake. Saloons, a hotel, and a few stores constituted the business district, and the population soon passed one hundred. With the collapse of copper prices in the 1920s, Old Hachita became a true ghost town and Hachita a dusty desert crossroads.

Old Hachita has a surprising number of surviving remnants enveloped in quintessential desert scenery. It is located at the end of a dusty, rocky unmarked road that is best found with inquiry in Hachita. Hachita is itself a fascinating stop. Two landmarks from the glory days are still in operation: the Hachita Saloon and the lovely St. Catherine of Sienna church.

## WHEN YOU GO

*From Lordsburg, drive east on Interstate 10 for 27 miles to exit 49. Turn south on State Highway 146 and continue for 19 miles.*

# STEINS

Steins Mountain is part of the Peloncillo Mountains along the Arizona and New Mexico border. One of the few springs in the area from which water flows throughout the year is located in the impressive mountain's shadow.

The mountain and spring were primary assets that led John Butterfield to construct a station here to serve his now legendary Butterfield Overland Stage Route, the route utilized by the first transcontinental mail and passenger service company. The Steins Peak station, as with most others built in New Mexico and Arizona, consisted of two stone and adobe rooms, each with a fireplace, and a stone corral in between. An earthen tank provided adequate storage for spring waters and the occasional rains.

In 1861, the American Civil War necessitated the removal of military patrols from the Southwest, which in turn sparked a resurgence in Apache raids. The Steins Peak station and most other stations in the area were abandoned, and the Butterfield line was rerouted north through Salt Lake City.

When the Southern Pacific Railroad arrived in southern New Mexico during the early 1890s, the springs at Steins Mountain and the pass through the mountains gained prominence once again. As the water stop became an important shipping center for area ranches, a small town developed.

Ruins may be protected from the ravages of vandals in Steins, New Mexico, but nothing can spare them from the harsh desert climate.

Steins is a rich tapestry of preservation, re-creation, and ruins, and visiting is a delightful opportunity to experience the lure of the ghost town without miles of dusty roads.

By the early years of the twentieth century, Steins' population had climbed to several hundred. The stores were well stocked, and the residents enjoyed a number of amenities not afforded to more isolated communities thanks to the railroad.

Steins quickly faded into obscurity with the conversion from steam power to diesel after World War II and the increased reliance on trucks with the improved highways. Today the structures that remain are either decaying, restored, or re-created and display remnants from the town's glory days.

## WHEN YOU GO

*From the Arizona border on Interstate 10, take exit 3 and drive north a half mile. For information about Steins and the hours the site is open for tours, call 505-542-9791.*

# ALMA

Today, Alma would need a few more buildings to even be considered a wide spot in the road. Most travelers zip through town on U.S. Highway 180 without a second glance at the quiet little community on the banks of the San Francisco River.

The community was never much larger back in its heyday, which is surprising in light of the role it played in the development of the New Mexico frontier. Moreover, its relative obscurity is also unusual because many famous and infamous individuals are associated with the town.

The founding of Alma was based upon dreams of a utopic world. As Maurice Coates, James Keller, and W. H. McCullough envisioned it, the little farming community along the San Francisco River in the foothills of the Mogollon Mountains would be a communal town that consisted a settlement of families and no saloons.

In 1878, Coates, Keller, and McCullough began plotting out the new town they christened Mogollon. That same year, Captain J. G. Birney purchased the whole endeavor and immediately changed the name to Alma in memory of his beloved mother.

The dreams of creating a peaceful farming community quickly faded. In 1879, an ambush and robbery claimed the lives of McCullough and Captain Birney. Then the next year James C. Cooney, a former quartermaster sergeant of the Eighth Cavalry stationed at Fort Bayard who discovered rich silver deposits in a canyon along Mineral Creek in the Mogollon Mountains, died in an Apache raid on Alma in 1880.

The threat of Indian raids provided only a small deterrent to determined prospectors eager to expand on Cooney's discovery and farmers who hoped to profit from the fertile fields that surrounded Alma. By mid-summer of 1883, Alma, according to a letter in the *Albuquerque Journal*, was "made up of thirty-five houses well constructed of adobe and lumber. We have two business houses doing general merchandising businesses, and in connection with the same a good salon and card rooms." With the development of mining communities, such as Mogollon, in the nearby mountains, the produce grown in Alma became a valuable commodity, as was the beef raised on area ranches.

Apache raiders raided the community again in 1883. The most prominent victims of this raid were Judge H. C. McComas of Silver City and his family.

History and legend associate numerous notables with Alma. William Antrim, stepfather to William Antrim (aka Billy the Kid), was supposedly a blacksmith in Alma. A ranch at Alma was the last stop for Butch Cassidy and his Wild Bunch associates before they relocated to Bolivia.

The original buildings from the community's glory days are now mere ruins, and the cemetery is overgrown. However, numerous vestiges dating to the earliest days of automobile use in the area remain.

## WHEN YOU GO

*From Silver City, follow U.S. Highway 180 north for 62 miles.*

# MOGOLLON

Mogollon, nestled within the narrow confines of Silver Creek Canyon, is a scenic wonder. The ruins have a rich patina of age and sit amidst a stunning setting of natural beauty, making this one of the most photogenic ghost towns in the Southwest.

Other prospectors may have discovered the silver-bearing ores in a canyon along Mineral Creek in the Mogollon Mountains, but Quartermaster Sergeant James C. Cooney of the Eighth Cavalry of Fort Bayard made them public knowledge. Despite the near constant threat of Apache attacks in the rugged, isolated mountains, Cooney declined an army commission in 1876 and returned to develop his find as a civilian.

As his claim developed and other prospectors arrived in the area, the small mining camp of Cooney, located a few miles north of present-day Mogollon, blossomed. Cooney enjoyed the profits of his find, but only for a short time. He died during an Apache raid in Alma during the spring of 1880.

Cooney's brother, Michael, assumed control of the mine and shepherded it through expansion and development. Meanwhile, larger deposits of silver and gold found south of Cooney and within the confines of Silver Creek Canyon sparked a parallel rush and the development of Mogollon.

The J. P. Holland General Store is an example of why Mogollon, New Mexico, ranks at the top of my favorite ghost town list.

Mogollon is squeezed into a narrow and scenic canyon of the Mogollon Mountains and is a photographer's delight.

By the late 1880s, Mogollon rapidly eclipsed Cooney, which was in a steep fall. A variety of stores, several hotels and churches, a theater, an ice plant, and numerous saloons and homes crowded the narrow canyon floor and cascaded up the canyon walls in Mogollon.

Floods and fires struck Mogollon several times, but the mountain mining town was rebuilt after each incident, each time more grand than the previous incarnation. After a period of unusually heavy rains in 1914, the tailings of the Little Fanny Mine on Fannie Hill slid to the canyon floor, dammed the creek, and created a lake that threatened to flood the center of the town. With heroic efforts, miners cleared the channel and saved Mogollon from complete annihilation.

Transportation was, and is, the primary problem in Mogollon. Today a paved, nine-mile road with grades in excess of 25 percent hairpin curves, precipitous drops, and single-lane spots in many places provides access. As late as 1915—the year the mines reached their zenith and the town consisted of more than two thousand residents—the ninety-mile trip to Silver City, the primary shipping point and supply center for the area, required ten days in severe weather. Teams of eighteen or twenty-four mules were the primary choice for freight haulers until 1917. The switch to trucks did not translate into faster service, due to the area's rugged terrain.

Mogollon has many ruins, with Silver Creek flowing along the main street and many buildings that require wooden bridges for access. Some of the highlights are a bed and breakfast housed in a renovated two-story adobe store built in 1885 and a delightful museum in another store across the street and creek. A few of the buildings were refaced or modified for the movie *My Name Is Nobody*, which was filmed in the early 1970s and starred Henry Fonda.

## WHEN YOU GO

*From Silver City, drive 58 miles west on U.S. Highway 180. Turn east on State Highway 159, and continue for 9 miles. The drive on Highway 159 is not for the timid, those pulling trailers, or oversized vehicles. The road is steep, contains hairpin curves, and is one lane in many places. During the winter months, it can be snowy and icy.*

# PINOS ALTOS

Henry Birch, Colonel Jacob Sniveley, and James Hicks—seasoned prospectors and veterans of the California Gold Rush—were panning for gold in the cool, pine-shaded waters of Bear Creek in May 1860 when Birch made a discovery of surprising richness. Their acquisition of supplies in Santa Rita, a mining community to the east, sparked a rush to the Bear Creek find, and soon hundreds of prospectors were working lode and placer finds.

The small, roughshod collection of dwellings became known as Birchville, in homage to Henry Birch. Birchville's isolation was a small deterrent compared to the threat of sporadic attacks by Apache raiders. One assault by an estimated four hundred raiders on September 22, 1861 resulted in an almost complete abandonment of the settlement.

The community began to flourish in 1867 with the establishment of Fort Bayard several miles to the south. A formal application for a post office under the name Pinos Altos (meaning tall pines) was filed that same year.

The Buckhorn Saloon in Pinos Altos, New Mexico, has met the needs of thirsty travelers and residents for more than 125 years.

The Methodist church in Pinos Altos, now an art gallery, was built with generous donations from the family of William Randolph Hearst, the publishing magnate.

The opera house in Pinos Altos, which is now a dinner theater and restaurant, blends seamlessly with the town's original structures, even though it is not even forty years old.

The establishment of Grant County by the territorial legislature and the appointment of Pinos Altos as the county seat in 1869 further fueled the town's prominence. By 1879, the business district included two hotels, clothing and general merchandise stores, a drug store, saloons, restaurants, and a barbershop.

The Hearst family, who was better known for its publishing empire, invested heavily in the community. The Methodist church, built in 1898, today is an art gallery and stands in testimony of this philanthropy.

The adobe store that now serves as an ice cream parlor and gift shop has some celebrity association. This building was originally the store owned by Sam and Roy Bean. Roy was a self-appointed judge in west Texas and became a larger-than-life figure famous for unusual rulings as "The Law West of the Pecos."

Pinos Altos' fall from prominence was a long one interspersed with bouts of promising discoveries. Its downward trend began with the transfer of the county seat to Silver City in 1871. The completion of a narrow gauge railroad from Silver City in 1906 made the mining of previously neglected low-grade ores profitable. An amazingly rich discovery at the Pacific Mine in 1911 sparked a new but brief rush.

By 1920, mining activity had declined to limited production at some of the major mines and individual placer mining in nearby streams. During the Great Depression, the latter became so popular that the town enjoyed another temporary resurgence.

Today, Pinos Altos is a mix of modern cabins, ruins among the towering pines, and historic structures that include the original adobe courthouse. Listed among the must-see sites are the Buckhorn Saloon, the opera house that hosts a melodramatic dinner theater, and the small museum.

PINOS ALTOS

## WHEN YOU GO

*From Silver City, drive 12 miles north on State Highway 15.*

# HANOVER, FIERRO, GEORGETOWN, AND SANTA RITA

These four towns share more than location—together they are the cornerstone for modern mining and one of the most overlooked chapters in the Southwest's mining history. All great mining discoveries seem to begin with a legend. This story begins with a pitched battle between soldiers under the command of Lieutenant Colonel Jose Manuel Carrasco, a band of Apache warriors in the valley of the Rio Mimbres, and copper-tipped arrows. Carrasco, the victor of that battle in 1800, was a native of a village on the Rio Tinto in Spain, which is known for its copper mines.

After resigning his commission, Carrasco and twenty-four companions returned to the Mimbres River Valley to find the source of the Apache copper. To their amazement, the copper they discovered was very pure and was literally lying on the ground in a vast field.

With funding from Don Manuel Francisco Elguea, a prominent banker, and a Criadero de Cobre land grant from the Spanish government, the miners began to develop mines and founded a small village they named Santa Rita.

Elguea negotiated a contract with the government to provide copper for coins to guarantee the endeavor's prosperity. In exchange, the government ensured low labor with the establishment of a penal colony at Santa Rita.

By 1805, more than five hundred men, many with families, called Santa Rita home. A steady stream of pack trains moving south to the refinery in Chihuahua with copper and north with goods from Mexico City allowed residents to enjoy a lifestyle seldom equaled on the frontier. Another rarity with settlers on the northern frontier was the community's peaceful relationship with neighboring Apaches.

However, a heinous event in 1837 changed everything. James Johnson, a trader and trapper, arrived in Santa Rita that year with the pretense of opening trading relations with the southern bands of Apaches. His true mission was to profit from the bounty on Apache scalps offered by the Mexican government, which was wisely overlooked by the people of Santa Rita. As bands of Apaches arrived on the appointed day for the trade fair, Johnson and his men sprung the trap with rifle and pistol fire. This pivotal attack sparked decades of warfare throughout the Southwest. The first target for the Apache was trappers on the Gila River. The second was the supply trains bound for Santa Rita. Within a year, the idyllic

The steel headframes and hoists at the mines in Hanover and Fierro are survivors from the communities' closing years as a mining center.

Many structures have been spared the destruction wrought by vandals in many abandoned mining towns, such as Hanover and Fierro, because the towns still have a small population.

world at Santa Rita was a distant memory. The Apache sought to remove the town from the face of the earth by burning many of the structures.

Santa Rita and the surrounding hills were full of riches. The mines at Santa Rita were again producing by 1841, and another discovery a few miles to the north led to the formation of another community, Fierro.

For the next forty years, both communities prospered, and additional finds in the area led to the establishment of Georgetown. Hanover was settled with completion of the railroad. With the exception of Georgetown, which was built on the discovery of rich silver deposits, these towns began to wane from prominence by 1885.

Georgetown was a community of red brick and mill-finished lumber buildings, unlike its neighbors where rough-cut wood and adobe were the building materials of choice. At its peak in 1890, the town had twelve hundred residents and a business district that included "two sawmills, a lumberyard, a leather works, [a] blacksmith, a wagon maker, a physician, [a] hospital, [a] drugstore, [a] bakery, [a] meat market, several dry goods stores, restaurants, a billiard parlor, [a] brewery, [a] jail, numerous saloons, and a hotel."

The collapse of silver catapulted Georgetown into a deep spiral of decline. Within twenty years, the town was little more than an historic footnote as most buildings were demolished with the materials used for construction in Silver City.

Affected to a lesser degree by the Panic of 1893 were Santa Rita, Hanover, and Fierro because the primary products from the mines in those communities were copper, gold, and iron. Still, by 1904, exhaustion of the accessible ores at Santa Rita led many to believe the old town in the shadow of the Kneeling Nun, a distinctive rock formation, was about to join Georgetown as a ghost town.

Enter John Sully, a brilliant and gifted engineer who attracted financial backers, purchased the mines and formed the Chino Copper Company in 1909. After completion of proper legal titles to the properties, Sully instituted a revolutionary new mining technology that transformed formerly unprofitable low grade ores into profitable ones by utilizing massive steam shovels to access ores. With this innovation, the era of open pit mining was born. This would be the final chapter for Santa Rita, however, for as the pit grew it transformed the town site into a deep hole.

Fierro and Hanover held on a bit longer, but the collapse of copper prices in the late 1920s and the onslaught of the Great Depression resulted of cessation of mining in 1931. Their resurrection during World War II was not enough to reconstitute the community; after the war, the mines again closed, a pattern of that continues to this day.

Only faded photos, a pleasant cemetery with ornate wrought-iron fencing, and mine tailings remain to mark Georgetown's place in history. The town site of Santa Rita is now an open pit mine of staggering dimensions. Fierro and Hanover, squeezed on both sides by towering mine tailings and precipitous mountains, are still home to a small number of residents and a surprisingly large number of original buildings as well as extensive ruins.

## WHEN YOU GO

*From Silver City, drive west on U.S. Highway 180 to the junction of State Highway 152, approximately 10 miles. Continue 6 miles to the junction with State Highway 366. A left turn at the junction provides access to Hanover and Fierro. Continue driving west on Highway 152 to the scenic overlook of the Santa Rita pit. Almost directly to the north of the highway is Forest Road 73, a graded gravel road. This road provides access to the Georgetown cemetery, about 2 miles farther, and the town site, an additional mile down the road.*

# ACKNOWLEDGMENTS

First and foremost I must thank my wife, who is my dearest friend, for her encouragement, patience, support, and prayers. Without these, none of this would have been possible.

I would be quite remiss if I did not thank Bob "Boze" Bell and the staff of *True West* magazine. Repeatedly that fine publication provided material for research, inspiration, and ideas.

Even though the author and photographer receive the accolades for books such as these, the editorial staff brings them to life. Without their polish and hard work, these books would most likely never be more than ideas transformed into rough-cut gems.

Last but not least I must thank the countless old-timers, pioneers, and storytellers who sparked the idea for this book more than forty years ago.

—J.H.

# ABOUT THE AUTHOR AND PHOTOGRAPHER

**AUTHOR JIM HINCKLEY** jokes that he has spent so much time in the deserts of the Southwest that he now qualifies as a dry roasted nut. This quip is followed by another about his inability to imagine living anywhere where trees obstruct the view, where temperatures are not at least one hundred degrees for three months of the year, and where rain is measured in anything other than inches. Storytellers, liars, and those who lived to tell the tales of life on the western frontier fueled his passion for the wild places of Arizona and New Mexico.

Jim's previous books include *The Big Book of Car Culture*, *Backroads of Arizona*, and *Route 66 Backroads*. He also writes a feature column, "Independent Thinker," for *Cars & Parts*, and numerous feature articles for *Route 66*, *American Road*, *Old Cars Weekly*, and *Hemmings Classic Car* magazines, the *Kingman Daily Miner*, and daily blog postings that chronicle the life of a starving artist on Route 66 at www.route66chronicles.blogspot.com. Jim resides in Kingman, Arizona, with his wife of twenty-six years, Judy, and two ancient cats.

**PHOTOGRAPHER KERRICK JAMES** took his Bachelor of Fine Arts in photography from Arizona State University in 1982. He has photographed the American West, Mexico, and the Pacific Rim for over twenty-five years. His work has appeared on more than two hundred book and magazine covers for *Arizona Highways*, *Alaska*, *National Geographic Adventure*, Voyageur Press, *Condé Nast Traveler*, *Outdoor Photographer*, *Sky*, *Sunset*, *Virtuoso Life*, and others.

Kerrick shot the photography for *Route 66 Backroads*, *Backroads of Arizona*, and *Our Arizona*. In addition to providing covers for two books by *National Geographic*, he has also shot guidebooks to the Southwest, Arizona, New Mexico, Las Vegas, and San Francisco for Compass American Guides. For Insight Guides, he has shot travel guides to Arizona, California, and San Francisco.

Kerrick teaches photo workshops throughout the year: trips on Cruise West vessels, which are sponsored by Pentax, and land-based workshops for Friends of Arizona Highways. He is a member of the Society of American Travel Writers, the Travel Journalist's Guild, and Through Each Other's Eyes. He lives in Mesa, Arizona, with his sons, Shane, Royce, and Keanu.